CONTENTS

Ships in Focus Publications

Correspondence and editorial:
Roy Fenton
18 Durrington Avenue
London SW20 8NT
0181 879 3527
rfenton@rfenton.demon.co.uk

Orders and photographic:
John & Marion Clarkson
18 Franklands, Longton
Preston PR4 5PD
01772 612855

Printed by Amadeus Press Ltd.,
Huddersfield.
Designed by Hugh Smallwood,
John Clarkson and Roy Fenton.
SHIPS IN FOCUS RECORD
ISBN 1 901 703 045

SHIPS IN FOC

Readers may notice
typography and layout of this e
notional third volume, we have m
text and photographs.

Several readers with marine engineering backgrounds
have written to request that we include more details of a ship's
machinery in captions to photographs and other descriptions.
This we are pleased to do, and we will encourage our other
authors to do likewise. We intend to confine this to main engines,
believing that listings of the type and catalogue number of every
generator, winch and radar set are best left to trade journals.
However, as non-engineers we would like to throw down a
challenge to marine engineer readers: please write us articles
which explain the differences between different types of
machinery. Even to non-specialists it is clear that diesel engines
differ markedly, with choices such as single- or double-acting,
two- or four- stroke cycles, although we would welcome
elucidation on just what these differences mean in terms of power
output, economy, reliability and maintenance requirements. But
as many of the ships which appear in these pages have triple-
expansion steam engines, what we would really like is some
comparisons of these. For instance, how and why did a steam
engine from North Eastern Marine Engineering differ from one of
similar power built by Central Marine Engine Works? From such
descriptions we would hope to gain a feel for the characteristics
expected from a particular engine builder, just as one develops a
feel for the outputs of different shipyards. So, engineers, to your
word processing machines.

The promised follow-up on Blue Funnel has been held
over until the next issue. Anyone with information further to or
amending that in *Ships in Focus: Blue Funnel Line* is invited to
get in touch. Not yet got a copy? Full details are opposite.
John Clarkson   Roy Fenton
                        June 1999

SUBSCRIPTION RATES FOR THREE ISSUES
Subscribers make a saving on the postage of three issues, and receive
each *Record* just as soon as it is published. They are also eligible for
concessions on newly-published *Ships in Focus* titles. Readers can
start their subscription with *any* issue, and are welcome to backdate
it to receive previous issues.

UK	£20	–
Europe (airmail)	£22	–
Rest of world (surface mail)	£22	US$36
Rest of world (airmail)	£30	US$49

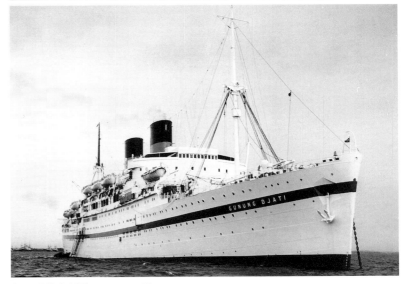

GUNUNG DJATI: see page 57
                [Col. Robert Gabriel, Ambrose Greenway collection]

DURHAM TRADER (2)
Austin and Pickersgill Ltd., Sunderland; 1959, 9,189gt, 478 feet

closed shelter decker, but her major external difference was the omission of the heavy lift derrick (see pages 11-12). She was

1954 merger with S.P. Austin and Son Ltd. DURHAM TRADER's career with her original owners was particularly short, however, and

Her second career was much longer than her first, and it was not until December 1983 that she arrived at Alang, India to be demolished.

TRADER NAVIGATION CO. LTD.

Although the international trade in cereals is only marginally less important than that in oil, those companies involved in the latter such as Shell and Esso are household names, whilst the names of grain traders are largely unknown to the general public. Indeed, even those knowledgeable about shipping would have difficulty naming the world's five big grain houses, although all have been extensive charterers and, to lesser extents, owners of ships. The grain business is dominated by companies which have both remained largely under the control of their founding families, and which cherish secrecy almost as highly as profitability.

To prosper, the grain merchant needs the intelligence to forecast how international markets are shaping; the ability to make arrangements with the government agencies which often buy and sell cereals; the courage to back its commercial judgements; and silos of money to fund its deals. These prerequisites have meant that the successful grain houses have seldom been challenged by newcomers, and the business has been dominated for many years by the same five names: André, Bunge, Cargill, Continental Grain, and Louis Dreyfus.

A large grain merchant may well be chartering a dozen or more ships each day, and all the five majors have at times offset the risk that freight rates may rise suddenly by controlling some of their own tonnage. Founded in Minneapolis in 1865, Cargill Incorporated were known in the north west of England for their CARCHESTER (9,074/1967) which traded almost all her life to the Brown and Polson mills at Manchester; her name being derived from CARgill + ManCHESTER. The other US-based major, Continental Grain of New York, had the LONDONER (9,306/1961) under the British flag in the 1960s and owned a number of tramps and bulkers under the United Steamship Corporation of Panama. In 1955 André et Cie. S.A. of Lausanne, itself dating from 1877, set up the largest Swiss shipowning company, Societé de Navigation Maritime Suisse-Atlantique S.A. Familiar to many readers will be Louis Dreyfus et Cie. S.A. of Paris, which once had important fleets under both the French and British flags (Buries Markes) and still retain ships, although they are now mostly flagged out. The fifth grain merchant, Bunge, is notable for having owned its entire fleet under the British flag, Trader Navigation: the subject of this article.

Bunge are an example of a trading house which has shifted its operations around the world in line with what it saw as its best interests. The Bunge family moved from Sweden to the Netherlands in the seventeenth century. Charles Bunge established himself as a trader in Amsterdam, but transferred the business to Antwerp in 1850 as the trade of that port grew. In Belgium, Eduardo Bunge became involved with King Leopold II's business interests in the Congo, which involved ruthless exploitation of both native peoples and natural resources. What really made Bunge's fortune, however, was their recognition that Argentina had the potential to become one of the world's great wheat producers. Following in his family's migratory traditions, Ernesto Bunge settled in Buenos Aires in the 1880s, just as the landowners of the Pampas were exploiting their vast holdings by letting them to tenant farmers. Bunge extended credit to these farmers, supplied their seed, and bought their wheat for export to Europe; thereby ensuring that Bunge profited as much as the landowners from the labours of the tenant farmers. Such was the importance of the River Plate grain trade to Bunge that their headquarters was established in Argentina. However, from Bunge's perspective the political situation in Argentina deteriorated after the Second World War, with President Juan Péron establishing a government monopoly of the cereal trade, and - after he had lost power - his supporters kidnapping and holding to ransom two senior Bunge executives. All this led the company to move again, this time to São Paolo in Brazil, although even today Bunge retains very considerable business interests in Argentina.

But in their heyday in the Plate trade around 1936, Bunge & Co. were chartering six to eight ships each day to move their grain. With the world slowly coming out of recession, they must have begun to fear that freight rates would not remain forever in the charterer's favour, and decided to build up a small fleet of their own. Trader Navigation Co. Ltd. was registered in London on 20th July 1936. The story of the gradual evolution of its modest fleet over the next 35 years is told in the captions accompanying the photographs. It is significant that, throughout its 35 years of shipowning, this international company which had shown no particular loyalty to any one country should retain its ships under the British flag and use nothing but British shipbuilders.

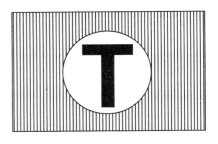

The funnel and flag of Trader Navigation Co. Ltd.: the basic colour of both was red. *[J.L. Loughran]*

ENGLISH TRADER

Furness Shipbuilding Co. Ltd., Haverton Hill-on-Tees; 1934, 3,953gt, 363 feet

ENGLISH TRADER was a fascinating, if singularly unlucky, ship. She was completed as ARCTEES, one of three ships built to demonstrate Sir Joseph Isherwood's novel Arcform hull design, and is shown as this on page 53 of *Record* 1. North Eastern Marine Engineering Co. Ltd. at Wallsend provided a set of their triple expansion engines for what was - aside from her revolutionary hull design and steel hatch covers – a typical long bridge-deck, coal-burning, nine-knot tramp.

Once Isherwood had demonstrated his Arcform principle (Lawther, Latta with their ANGLO-INDIAN (5,609/1937) were one of the few owners he persuaded to adopt it) the three ARCs were sold, and in 1936 ARCTEES became Trader Navigation's first ship, their only ENGLISH TRADER. It is not surprising that they never used the name again. On only her second voyage for the new owners, she went aground off

Dartmouth on 23rd January 1937. In the top photograph opposite, an unsuccessful attempt to refloat her involves (left to right) the naval tug RETORT, the Dutch WITTE ZEE, HMS WITCH, and a Dartmouth harbour tug.

The pounding strained her hull so badly that she showed signs of breaking up between numbers 1 and 2 holds. It was therefore decided to complete the job by cutting away the fore part and abandoning it (opposite middle, taken 22nd February 1937). The unusual Arcform hull cross section shows to good effect in the photograph of the refloated ENGLISH TRADER (opposite bottom).

In April 1937 the ship was towed to Southampton to be drydocked for temporary repairs. The top photograph shows the difficulties of towing stern first: the ENGLISH TRADER is shearing so badly that the tow rope is almost at right angles to her hull.

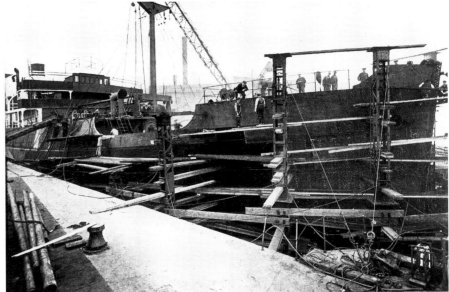

From Southampton ENGLISH TRADER was taken to the Tyne for a new bow section to be fitted by Middle Docks Engineering Co. Ltd. at South Shields. Once she arrived on the Tyne, work proceeded briskly: despite the fact that, with her Arcform hull, almost every plate had to be rolled, the new bow was plated up within three weeks (right, taken on 21st September 1937).

ENGLISH TRADER went back to work, and on 26th October 1941 she left London on charter to British India for a voyage that was due to take her to Table Bay and Mombasa with general cargo. But she got no farther than Hammond Knoll on the Norfolk coast where, in a full north north east gale, she drove ashore and her situation quickly became desperate. Five men were swept overboard and lost, and the rescue of the 44 survivors became one of the epic stories of the lifeboat service. At 8.15 am the Cromer lifeboat H.F. BAILEY was launched under the redoubtable Coxswain Henry Blogg, perhaps the most decorated lifeboatman ever, who later said that the ENGLISH TRADER was the worst problem he had ever faced. The H.F. BAILEY took over three hours to reach the scene, by which time the ENGLISH TRADER's hull was almost under water. After an attempt to fire a rocket line aboard failed, the lifeboat stood off until 2.15 pm, but a second attempt to get close to the wreck resulted in disaster. The H.F. BAILEY capsized, and five men including the 65-year old Henry Blogg were thrown into the water, although fortunately all five were rescued. Undaunted, Blogg and his crew went out again at 4.15 am the next morning, and this time rescued the 44 men still on board. As if in shame, the ENGLISH TRADER sank into the Norfolk sands, and remains there, covered to a depth of three metres. [All Derek Blackhurst collection, except bottom left: Laurence Dunn collection]

WELSH TRADER (1) (top and middle) and
BETELGEUZE (bottom)
*Joseph L. Thompson and Sons Ltd.,
Sunderland; 1938, 4,974g, 442 feet*
Despite their unhappy experience with the
ENGLISH TRADER at the beginning of 1937,
Trader Navigation soon ordered larger but
more conventional steamers, although with
a composite, rather than split,
superstructure. WELSH TRADER emerged
from the Wear in March 1938, the Wallsend
works of North Eastern Marine Engineering
Co. (1938) Ltd. providing triple-expansion
steam engines to drive her at a modest nine
knots.

WELSH TRADER lived up to her name, and
made several visits to Cardiff. In 1951 she was
sold to 'Orion' Schiffahrt Ges. Reith & Co. K.G.,
of Hamburg who, in their tradition of naming
ships after stars and constellations, renamed
her BETELGEUZE. In 1961 she passed to
Italian owners, who proved there was still
economic life left in an ageing nine-knot tramp
steamer, and as PEPPINO PALOMBA she
survived until 22nd May 1970 when she arrived
at La Spezia for demolition. *[Top and middle:
courtesy William Schell]*

SCOTTISH TRADER (1) (opposite top)
*Joseph L. Thompson and Sons Ltd.,
Sunderland; 1938, 4,016g, 406 feet*
The second of the initial pair from
Sunderland, SCOTTISH TRADER was
smaller than WELSH TRADER, probably
reflecting the owners desire to find the
optimum design. In fact, SCOTTISH
TRADER proved more suitable for the River
Plate trade than the WELSH TRADER, and at
the time was probably the biggest vessel
that could load a full cargo of grain at the
up-river ports.

SCOTTISH TRADER's career was short and tragic. She left Philadelphia on 15th November 1941 for Liverpool with steel and foodstuffs and - after sailing from Sydney, Nova Scotia on 22nd November - was last reported on 3rd December. She and her crew disappeared, and only when German records were examined after the war was it learned that she had been torpedoed by U 131 somewhere south of Iceland on 6th December 1941. With the ENGLISH TRADER wrecked in October, the company had now lost two of its three ships within six weeks. *[Ivor Rooke collection]*

MIDDLESEX TRADER (1) (below)
Joseph L. Thompson and Sons Ltd., Sunderland; 1942, 7,241g, 441 feet
Trader Navigation's losses persuaded the Ministry of War Transport to allocate them two newbuildings, and although they came from the yard the company had favoured pre-war, they were to standard 'B' type designs, albeit incorporating a few of the owner's features. However, the two heavy lift derricks visible in this post-war view of MIDDLESEX TRADER were hardly necessary in the grain trade. Both ships had triple-expansion engines built by George Clark (1938) Ltd. at Sunderland.

MIDDLESEX TRADER went aground in the St. Lawrence on 16th July 1955, remaining thus until the 31st July, and the extensive damage seems to have precipitated her disposal, as she was sold later that year to London-Greek owners A. Lusi Ltd. They renamed her STROVILI and put her under the Costa Rican flag, which was enjoying a brief period of popularity as a flag of convenience. Her tenure here was short, and later that year she went to Holland as ANKER for N.V. Anker Kolen Maatschappij of Rotterdam. Her final owners were Italian, and she ran as CARNIA from 1958 to March 1963 when she was laid up at La Spezia, from which she emerged to be broken up in Italy in 1964. *[Fotoflite incorporating Skyfotos]*

ESSEX TRADER (1) (top) and **ESKCLIFFE** (middle)

Joseph L. Thompson and Sons Ltd., Sunderland; 1943, 7,237g, 441 feet

The second war-built steamer was distinguishable from MIDDLESEX TRADER by the lack of heavy lift gear. Internally, she had three boilers rather than two, giving her a marginally better performance. Like her sister, ESSEX TRADER retained her war rig of tall signal mast amidships but no topmasts long after the war. Indeed, the removal of the barrel-like crow's nest is the only alteration visible in the photograph of her as ESKCLIFFE, taken in Vancouver after her 1957 sale to Esk Shipping Co. Ltd. This company had a rather interesting history, being a 1955 renaming of the Chellew

Navigation Co. Ltd., itself a long-established Cornish-owned tramping company. Esk Shipping had as its principal investor Howard M. Lund, a member of an old-established Whitby shipowning family, although then based in London. As a late attempt to revive tramp shipping under the British flag it was not particularly successful. ESKCLIFFE remained with the company only until 1960, and by 1964 its deepsea tramps had gone, although Howard Lund subsequently owned a fleet of coastal motorships.

The ship spent the last eight years of her life, from 1960 to 1967, as the Panama-flag SANDRA trading in the Far East for C.S. Koo of Hong Kong. She was broken up at Kaohsiung in 1967. [Fotoflite incorporating Skyfotos, and World Ship Photo Library collection]

SUSSEX TRADER (1) (opposite bottom)
Sir James Laing and Sons Ltd., Sunderland; 1947, 4,221gt, 391 feet
In his history of Trader Navigation published in *Marine News* of July 1963, Managing Director C.F. Godwin was rather dismissive of the SUSSEX TRADER's performance suggesting that, as a handy-sized ship, she suffered from competition with Liberty types (which were significantly bigger) and spent most of her career on charter until sold in 1954, after only seven years' service. An alternative explanation is that her steam engines, built once again by North Eastern Marine Engineering Co. (1938) Ltd., were something of an anachronism when she was built in 1947. Her next owners, Malabar

Steamship Co. Ltd., got more service out of her, but as JANANI she was laid up in her home port of Bombay in October 1962, going to Indian breakers almost a year later. [Fotoflite incorporating Skyfotos]

DURHAM TRADER (1) (bottom) and GLENWOOD (middle)
Sir James Laing and Sons Ltd., Sunderland; 1940, 4,897gt, 415 feet
Trader Navigation showed a remarkable loyalty to the products of Sunderland shipbuilders, ordering all but one of their newbuildings from the Wear and acquiring this one secondhand. She had been built as GLENWOOD for John I. Jacobs and Co. Ltd. of London, a company which in post-war years became better known for their tankers.

Machinery was also familiar: a steam engine built by North Eastern Marine Engineering Co. (1938) Ltd.

On acquisition in 1948 she was renamed DURHAM TRADER. Sale in 1957 saw her joining the expanding Indian merchant fleet as the JAG SEVAK for Great Eastern Shipping Co. Ltd., founded in Bombay in 1948. She had the dubious distinction of becoming the first loss sustained by this company. On 15th July 1965 JAG SEVAK was leaving Visakhapatnam with cement and general cargo when she stranded and was so badly damaged that she was declared a constructive total loss. [Middle: National Museums and Galleries of Wales, 909/1015; bottom: Fotoflite incorporating Skyfotos]

SCOTTISH TRADER (2) (top) and **BANNERCLIFF** (bottom)
Lithgows Ltd., Port Glasgow; 1948, 5,590gt, 437 feet

The second SCOTTISH TRADER was the only ship the company owned which was not built on Wearside, and one of only two engines-amidships vessels not to have the rather anachronistic split superstructure. The company's first motorship, SCOTTISH TRADER had a Doxford four-cylinder two-stroke built by David Rowan and Co. Ltd. Perhaps surprisingly in view of her more economical machinery, she did not last much longer with the company than contemporary steamers, and was sold in 1960 to the North Shipping Co. Ltd. who renamed her NORTH CAMBRIA. This name

was a reminder that her managers, Hugh Roberts and Son, had their origins in North Wales and were most unusual in migrating not to Cardiff or Liverpool to begin shipowning but to Newcastle-upon-Tyne.

In 1963 a further sale saw this motorship become BANNERCLIFF, retaining British registry but owned in Bermuda by the Bond Shipping Co. Ltd. This was under the control of a London-Greek company, Adelphi Vergottis Ltd., a relatively minor arm of a shipowning family of some age and distinction. Unusually, Adelphi Vergottis used a different funnel for his British-flag ships from that on his flag-of-convenience vessels: a V for Vergottis combined with Bs denoting Bond and

Banner, the names of his companies.

In 1970, the ship became the SILVER COAST under the Cypriot flag and ownership of Panos Daifos, and in 1973 the GRANIKOS. Within a few months of this sale, on 1st November, she caught fire after an engine room explosion whilst discharging fertiliser at Nuevitas in Cuba. She was beached and the fire extinguished, but in view of her 25 years she was declared a compromised total loss, and was towed to Santander in Spain for breaking up, where she arrived on 6th April 1974. *[Both: Fotoflite incorporating Skyfotos]*

WELSH TRADER (2) (top), **ROOKLEY** (middle upper), **LONDON BREEZE** (middle lower) and **GOLDEN BRIDGE** (bottom).

William Pickersgill and Sons Ltd., Sunderland; 1954, 5,671gt, 447 feet

The WELSH TRADER of 1954 introduced a distinctive appearance to the fleet, with the traditional split superstructure trunking number three hold, and complemented by a rather large funnel. The four ships built to this layout over a four-year period showed a significant increase in size but, despite detail differences, formed a readily-recognised group. All had the same Doxford-type oil engines as their immediate predecessor, but this time all were built by North Eastern Marine Engineering Co. Ltd. at Wallsend.

WELSH TRADER had a subtle curve to her bow lacking in the later three ships, and a particularly large funnel, whose proportions were not helped by a rather bulbous cowl top. This made her distinctive throughout her life, as the photographs demonstrate. After only seven years' service, Trader Navigation sold her in 1961 to Stephens, Sutton Ltd. who renamed her ROOKLEY. The photograph of her as ROOKLEY is relatively rare, as within two years the Newcastle-upon-Tyne company disposed of her, together with their RIPLEY (5,843/1953), to John Manners and Co. Ltd. of Hong Kong, who gave ROOKLEY the name LONDON BREEZE. Manners were building up an impressive fleet at the time, much of it employed on charter to the People's Republic of China and to Indonesia, and LONDON BREEZE was soon seen back in UK waters, and again photographed by Skyfotos. In 1970 she was sold to other Hong Kong owners, and ran under various flags as GOLDEN BRIDGE until 1977, when she went to the Vietnamese Government as SONGHUONG (the name SONG THU BON was also reported for her). Simply as SONG she arrived at Taiwan for breaking up in June 1980. *[Top: World Ship Photo Library; middle photos: Fotoflite incorporating Skyfotos]*

SUSSEX TRADER (2) (top), **HERBERT MACAULAY** (middle) and **ANEL D'AZUR** (bottom)
William Pickersgill and Sons Ltd., Sunderland; 1957, 6,041gt, 460 feet
Second of the Pickersgill group, SUSSEX TRADER showed some detail differences to her superstructure, but most notable was a more restrained funnel and an additional pair of kingposts aft.

The full cargo gear of these open shelter deckers, which included a heavy lift derrick on the foremast, strongly suggests they were built as much for charter to liner companies as for the grain trade, and after rather short careers with Trader Navigation several did become cargo liners. In 1964 SUSSEX TRADER joined the growing fleet of Nigerian National Shipping Line Ltd., spending 12 years on their routes as HERBERT MACAULAY. Sale in 1976 saw her become the Panamanian ANEL D'AZUR, which was broken up on Gadani Beach in August 1982. *[Top and middle: A. Duncan courtesy World Ship Photo Library collection]*

ESSEX TRADER (2) (top) and **SAFINA-E-ISMAIL** (middle)
William Pickersgill and Sons Ltd., Sunderland; 1958, 5,902gt, 465 feet
The second ESSEX TRADER was an almost exact repeat of the SUSSEX TRADER, differing only in being slightly longer and deeper, although of smaller gross tonnage. The shelter decks on the first three of this group were closed in 1960, dramatically increasing their tonnage: ESSEX TRADER, for instance, being remeasured at 8,455gt.

In 1963 ESSEX TRADER was sold to the Pan-Islamic Steamship Co. Ltd. of Karachi to become SAFINA-E-ISMAIL, as which she is seen at Chittagong on 14th August 1987. This company's name reflected investment by muslims in both Pakistan and Saudi Arabia, but did not prevent it being nationalised by the Pakistani Government in 1974. SAFINA-E-ISMAIL traded on without change of name, however, and only after an impressive 24 years under this second name was she broken up at Gadani Beach, arriving in December 1987. *[Fotoflite incorporating Skyfotos and Michael Pryce courtesy World Ship Photo Library collection]*

SCOTTISH TRADER (3) (bottom)
Austin and Pickersgill Ltd., Sunderland; 1962, 11,563gt, 507 feet
The short career of the second DURHAM TRADER showed that the future of the grain trade lay with bulk carriers, and Trader Navigation's first venture into this field was the Sunderland-built SCOTTISH TRADER. Interestingly, she was equipped with the same type of oil engine that was fitted to the second SCOTTISH TRADER 14 years earlier, although the example in the bulk carrier was built by the designers themselves, William Doxford and Sons (Engineers) Ltd. of Sunderland.

However, the SCOTTISH TRADER's career with Trader Navigation was to be almost as short as the conventional ships which had preceded her, and in 1968 she was sold to become FEDERAL TYNE of the oddly-named Random Ltd. Managers were the old-established Burnett Steamship Co. Ltd. of Newcastle-upon-Tyne, but her name strongly points to ultimate ownership by Federal Commerce and Navigation Co. Ltd. of Montreal. She appears to have remained under charter to Federal after 1971 when she passed to Swiss owners who put her under the Panama flag as FEDERAL SALSO. After 1978 sales and renamings followed thick and fast: ROZELBAY in 1978, GIUCA in 1982, and JAMBI in 1983, as which she arrived at Saki, Japan in August 1985 to be broken up. *[Fotoflite incorporating Skyfotos]*

MIDDLESEX TRADER (2) (opposite top)
Austin and Pickersgill Ltd., Sunderland;
1963, 14,083gt, 583 feet
The design of SCOTTISH TRADER was
stretched for the final three ships of Trader
Navigation. Apart from the extra hatch and
additional derricks to serve it, MIDDLESEX
TRADER is externally quite similar to her
immediate predecessor. Internally,
however, the company had finally deserted
Doxford to fit a Gotaverken-designed diesel,
a six-cylinder two-stroke manufactured on
the Tyne by North Eastern Marine
Engineering Co. Ltd.

Her career with Trader Navigation was, like
her sisters, sadly brief, and in 1969 she was
sold to Greek owners who named her
HOMER, although this became ASSIOS in
1970. Her most notable owner in the post-
Trader Navigation period was the Peruvian
company, Negocios del Mar S.A., who owned
her as POLLUX from 1978 until 1984, when she
went back under a flag-of-convenience,
becoming the Maltese POLO. Far Eastern
shipbreakers ran amok amongst this group of
bulkers in 1985 and 1986, and POLO arrived at
Alang to meet her fate in March 1985.
[Fotoflite incorporating Skyfotos]

SURREY TRADER (opposite middle)
Austin and Pickersgill Ltd., Sunderland;
1964, 14,064gt, 583 feet
SURREY TRADER was identical to
MIDDLESEX TRADER externally and in her
machinery. She also managed only six
years with Trader Navigation, before being
sold to become SATURN. A reminder of the
origins of Trader Navigation in the River
Plate grain trade came in 1979 with her sale
as CORAJE to Nobleza Maritime S.A. of
Montevideo at the mouth of the self-same
river. This small company's three ships
were all ex-British owned and built, the
other two being coasters. CORAJE arrived
at Xinjang, China to be demolished in March
1985. *[Fotoflite incorporating Skyfotos]*

VANCOUVER TRADER, ex-ESSEX TRADER
(3) (opposite bottom)
Austin and Pickersgill Ltd., Sunderland;
1968, 13,953gt, 583 feet
Photos of the company's last ship, the third
ESSEX TRADER, under her original name
have proved elusive. She was a near-sister
to the MIDDLESEX and SURREY TRADERs,
differing only in having machinery built at
Gothenburg by A/B Gotaverken.

In 1971 Bunge and Co. Ltd. finally decided to
quit shipowning, and Trader Navigation Co.
Ltd., along with its last surviving ship ESSEX
TRADER, was sold to August Leffler & Son
A/B of Gothenburg. Management remained
in the UK, with Denholms of Greenock, but
she was renamed VANCOUVER TRADER.
This name lasted until 1979 when she was
sold and hoisted the Panama flag under the
rather meaningless name NEW FUTURE.
After a further sale in 1982 she became
merely FUTURE, and in November 1986
arrived at Alang to be broken up. It is
interesting to note that she was survived by
just one of her original owner's ships, the
former ESSEX TRADER (2). *[National
Museums and Galleries of Wales, 4510/iv]*

EMPIRE ISEULT as **FRANS VAN MIERIS**
(top) and **FARMSUM** (middle)
Joseph L. Thompson and Sons Ltd.,
Sunderland; 1942, 7,170gt, 442 feet
With their close relationship with Joseph L.
Thompson and Sons Ltd., it is not surprising
that Trader Navigation were asked to
supervise and then manage a wartime
standard ship built by this Sunderland yard.
Management was short-lived, however, as
in 1943 EMPIRE ISEULT was transferred to
the ownership of the Dutch Government in
exile in London and renamed FRANS VAN
MIERIS after a Dutch artist, with
management passing to the Netherlands
Shipping and Trading Committee Ltd. After
the war, the ship remained with Dutch
managers Vinke & Co. as FARMSUM. In
1959 she was sold east, becoming the Hong
Kong-owned KIN MIANG and in 1965 the
Taiwan-owned KAI QUEN. She was broken
up at Kaohsiung in September 1969. *[Top:
National Maritime Museum; middle:
Fotoflite incorporating Skyfotos, both
courtesy of World Ship Photo Library
collection]*

FORT GLENORA (bottom)
West Coast Shipbuilders Ltd., Vancouver,
Canada; 1943, 7,126gt, 425 feet
Trader Navigation managed a Canadian-
built Fort-type steamer for the Ministry of
War Transport, a ship whose design also
originated with Joseph L. Thompson and
Sons Ltd. FORT GLENLORA was managed
from completion in May 1943 until 1946. By
the time this photograph was taken on 24th
June 1950 she was under the management
of Stott, Mann and Fleming Ltd. of
Newcastle-upon-Tyne, but her appearance
probably differed little from her wartime
years, with no topmasts and a tall
radio/signal mast on the bridge. Soon
afterwards, she was sold to N.G. Kyriakides
Shipping Co. Ltd. with whom she remained
under the British flag as GEORGE K. In 1956
she went under the Liberian flag as
AFRICAN MARQUIS, but on 25th February
1958 ran aground on Kassos Island, off the
coast of Crete whilst on a voyage from
Morphou Bay to Hamburg. She
subsequently broke in two and sank. *[G.A.
Osbon, World Ship Photo Library]*

The second DUNEDIN STAR [Fotoflite incorporating Skyfotos]

THE TWO DUNEDIN STARS
Captain A.W. Kinghorn

The first DUNEDIN STAR was built at Birkenhead during 1935/6, one of that remarkable class of eight 11,000-ton, twin-screw, 12 passenger, refrigerated motor ships which swept Blue Star Line into the Commonwealth Conference in the face of fierce opposition. The well-entrenched Shaw Savill & Albion (acquired in 1935 by the Furness group), New Zealand Shipping Company/Federal Lines under the control of P&O, and the Commonwealth & Dominion Line, which became Port Line in 1937 and was the Australasian arm of Cunard, were not amused. Big guns!

But the Vestey family not only owned Blue Star Line together with much of the Australian and New Zealand beef, hides, sheepmeats and wool carried, but were very determined, combining sound financial stability with a gift for putting the right people in the right place at the right time, to oversee their operations ashore and afloat. The eight new ships were followed in 1939 by the very similar, but slightly larger AUCKLAND and WELLINGTON STARs. These 16-knots-plus refrigerated cargo carriers made a substantial contribution to Britain's war effort, six of them being lost in the conflict. Their full story is told in an accompanying feature.

Personal interest

The family were also keenly interested in the ships for their own sakes, making frequent personal inspections. It is no exaggeration to say they loved their ships, a sentiment which filtered down through their seafaring employees to all levels. The captain would be advised that Mr Vestey was coming down at 7.00 next morning, at which time he, the chief engineer, and the chief officer, in full uniform, would be present on the gangway when their smartly dark-suited, bowler-hatted employer stepped out of his chauffeur-driven car. After a brisk 'Good morning gentlemen,' he walked purposefully right around the ship followed by a puffing entourage of superintendents and ship's officers. The forecastle head came first and woe betide the mate who had neglected to paint his hawse pipes and windlass! Forward hatches came next with pertinent questions about the cargo therein, before the procession proceeded aft, to include inspection of the steering flat. After the monkey island and bridge it was time for breakfast in the saloon, followed by the chief engineer taking him round the engine room. A smart, efficiently-run ship, well painted without and within, was mandatory, while the owners insisted at all times, of course, on the good old-fashioned maxim - No Waste! That the Vesteys have survived in owning refrigerated ships right through the turmoil of modern times, when all the others except for P&O itself have long gone, is a testimony to their enthusiasm and business acumen.

DUNEDIN STAR came to grief on 29th November 1942. Outward bound from Liverpool to the Middle East, packed with war material for the British Forces defending Egypt and 21 passengers (extras were permitted in wartime) she was to have called first at Cape Town, but struck bottom off the west coast of South Africa and was beached to save her from sinking. Sailing under Admiralty orders, without radar and with a defective echo sounder, she must have been swept inshore by the unpredictable currents with which that always dangerous and unlit coast is fraught. Cast up in one of the world's most desolate places, there was, amazingly, no loss of life or serious injury amongst her 100 plus people. As a result of heroic efforts by various rescue parties, 4,000 bags of mail for the troops and some 300 tons of cargo were also saved. John Marsh and Lynam Anson's Pan book, *Skeleton Coast,* vividly describes this shipwreck and its dramatic aftermath.

Though she could hardly be described as having been a lucky ship, that no-one was lost in her stranding when so many others were perishing in the rigours of wartime meant there can have been little hesitation in retaining the name for a post-war vessel; unlike ARANDORA STAR which sank under such tragic circumstances in 1940 that the name was never used again.

The second DUNEDIN STAR

Thus the name of that Edinburgh-over-the-Sea, which in the Gaelic is Dunedin, was chosen in 1950 for a ship still on the stocks at Alexander Stephens' Linthouse yard, bought from Moller's Lancashire Shipping Company for whom she was to have been the BOLTON CASTLE. She was, in fact, the last ship that company would order, a single screw turbine steamer of 7,322 gross tons designed to carry general cargo in her six holds, and 12 first class passengers. Following Mollers' custom she would have had British officers and Chinese ratings, the former housed amidships with the passengers, the latter aft.

During her fitting out Blue Star rearranged the accommodation to suit a completely British complement of 57, with officers and ratings all being housed amidships, and only one two-berth passenger cabin. The original Chinese crew accommodation was converted into extra cargo space and storerooms. Her raked straight plate stem was pierced with a now-plated-over third hawsepipe, which, with space for a much larger windlass, would have been used when lying to buoys in the harbours of the Far East. Windlass and all winches were electric, while main propulsion power was from Foster Wheeler boilers supplying steam to three Parson's turbines geared to the single screw. Normal running speed was 16 knots, on around 40 tons of oil fuel and 20 tons of

DUNEDIN STAR on the Mersey, 14th October 1950. She still carries her Moller's main topmast, and her bulwarks are painted black.

fresh water daily, for all purposes.

Decks on the monkey island, bridge, captain's deck, and boat deck were sheathed with pitch pine and the rather old-fashioned space between bridge and funnel was largely occupied by No. 3 hatches – a large centre hatch and two smaller wing hatches. These wing hatches were covered with tarpaulins in the traditional manner, but all other upper deck cargo hatches had individual-pull, sliding steel MacGregors.

Originally she was to have four aluminium lifeboats, two under the bridge and two abreast the funnel, but with a smaller crew and just two passengers, only the after pair of boats was retained, slung under quadrantal luffing davits. Instead of petrol or diesel engines, these boats were 'mechanically propelled' by hand-operated Fleming Gear, in which the boat's occupants worked the upright vertical hand levers cranked to a propeller shaft, which was capable of driving the boat along at the required speed of four knots.

The funnel must have been the company's tallest, measuring 46 feet in height from the fiddley top (measured by the third mate, Ian MacKillop and myself), with an oval cross section 70 feet in circumference. The fresh water and sanitary salt water header tanks were situated high in the funnel, which always ensured a good pressure but which, of course, had to be taken into account when calculating the vessel's stability. Although she had two masts, only the foremast carried a topmast, in keeping with the single-masted current Blue Star custom. But unlike in the other single-masted liners where the forward white steaming light had to be rigged on the forestay, the DUNEDIN STAR had her mainmast light atop the funnel, with the forward light suitably sited on the foremast.

During 1956 No. 2 and No. 3 lower holds and 'tween decks were fitted to carry refrigerated cargo by insulating the steel sides, decks and deckheads with slab cork and fibreglass, cladded over with timber which was painted in special brown insulation varnish (other ships had white varnished insulated cargo spaces). Refrigeration machinery was installed in the enlarged engine room and cold air was blown through the cargo by powerful electric fans via ducted trunking. The remaining two-passenger cabin was taken over by a refrigeration engineer officer. All other cargo spaces, including Nos. 2 and 3 shelter decks, remained uninsulated for the carriage of general cargo.

Chief Officer

Having obtained my master's certificate in April 1960, I was appointed DUNEDIN STAR's chief officer two months later – my first ship as first mate. By this time she was ten years old – the best age to be for a ship of that type. All the teething troubles which inevitably beset any ship have been overcome, her machinery has been properly run in, yet rust and decay have not had time to take hold, provided that adequate maintenance has been applied throughout her life. When I joined in London's Royal Victoria Dock, I found the upper, flat capping-surface of all the ship's side bulwarks was painted black, which contrasted rather well – her previous mate thought – with the inboard yellow and black steel decks. But Mr Vestey had asked: 'For whom are we in mourning' and I was told very firmly by Captain Dickers, the Marine Superintendent, that white was the colour - to match the outside of the bulwarks - and that was that! But interior paint schemes were less rigid, and although the company colour for cabins was ivory gloss, nobody protested when my cabin arrived home in Liverpool a delicate shade of duck-egg blue with flat white deckhead.

DUNEDIN STAR had comfortable accommodation, bearing in mind that this was before air-conditioning and panelled deckheads. I had a large cabin with double bunk and private bathroom, situated on the port side of the deck below the bridge, abaft the captain who occupied the whole of the foreside. Second and third mates' and a double cadet's cabin were to starboard, while the senior

DUNEDIN STAR's first call at the port after which she was named: 6th February 1952. [Ian Farquhar collection]

DUNEDIN STAR off Circular Quay, Sydney during the 1950s. A British Phosphate Commission ship is alongside the quay on the left, and right is a two-funnelled passenger ship, the Dutch JOHAN VAN OLDENBARNEVELT (19,921/1930). [Author]

cadet had what was formerly the fourth mate's room, next to mine. Engineers occupied what Mollers had intended to be the passenger accommodation deck, with the ratings and petty officers below in single and two-berth cabins on the main deck. In very hot weather with a following wind I usually slept out on deck in a canvas hammock - more comfortable, and healthier.

Antipodean voyages

I made two voyages in the DUNEDIN STAR: the first out to Australia and home via Suez; and the second with a full general cargo out from London to Curacao for bunkers, through the Panama Canal to Fiji and New Zealand. Then, on to load in Hobart, Geelong, Newcastle NSW, Sydney, and Brisbane, where we lifted the first ever big shipment of Queensland apples – 50,000 cases – for Liverpool. That voyage we also loaded frozen lamb, mutton and beef; cartons of frozen egg pulp; bales of wool and sheepskins; sacks of rice and sacks of flour; wet hides; cartons of tinned meat and fruit; drums of neatsfoot oil; and – Australia's oldest export – drums of eucalyptus oil. Also at Brisbane, 132 bags of mail for Singapore, and one live dog for Liverpool. This cargo was for discharge at Dunkirk, Liverpool, Antwerp, Bremen, Hamburg and London – from Brisbane, calling at Singapore, Aden, Suez, and Gibraltar – a typical voyage of those days in that type of ship. 'Round the World and home again!'

She was a handy ship, a useful, versatile member of the fleet, and was always considered one of the best to sail in. Well laid out, both on deck and below, her engine room was always a model of cleanliness and efficiency, while the funnel was tall enough to throw the inevitable soot from daily tube-blowing well clear of her spotless decks. Although she had a reliable gyro compass this did not incorporate auto-steering, unlike most other Blue Star vessels, even those of 1935 vintage. However, the extra seamen needed for steering were also most useful in port when it came to covering hatches against a sudden shower of rain. In those days we had enough men to cover the job adequately, all the time.

When in Sydney on my second voyage, great interest was aroused by the stranding on Middleton Reef of the Shaw Savill liner, RUNIC (13,587/1950), whilst on passage from Brisbane, where she had completed unloading, to Auckland, where she would load. Thus she was light ship when she struck the reef, which lies low in the water probably below radar scan, at full sea speed about 01 30 on Sunday, 19th February 1961. Her SOS was answered by Chapman's tramp, BRIGHTON (6,073/1960), of Newcastle-on-Tyne. Two tugs set out for the wreck from Sydney and Brisbane, while the destroyer, HMAS VENDETTA, took off several of the crew and landed them in Sydney. One third of her 561-feet length was hard and fast on the reef, making salvage impossible. She was still there ten years later, and probably her remains are visible yet. Another fine ship lost to powerful and unpredicted currents.

Later career

DUNEDIN STAR was kept on the Southern Dominions run – with general cargo out from the UK and Europe, primary produce homeward (and all long before the EEC!) – until June 1968, when she was transferred within the Vestey Group to Lamport and Holt, of Liverpool, and renamed ROLAND. Employed on their old-established service from the

Apples from Brisbane in number 2 'tween deck of DUNEDIN STAR at Liverpool in 1961: Chief Officer Kinghorn (right) in discussion with a representative of the Australian Fruit Board and Second Officer Don MacNeil. In the shelter deck above is wool for Antwerp, canned meat and eucalyptus oil. [Author]

UK to the east coast of South America, in 1969 she was chartered to Frota Oceanica Brasileira for their inaugural voyage from South America to South Africa, Singapore, Hong Kong and Japan. Thus, at last, she found herself in the Far East, the trading area for which Mollers had originally laid her down.

Resuming her UK-River Plate trading after this far eastern sojourn, ROLAND was sold to a Cypriot owner in 1975, renamed JESSICA and registered in Limassol. By now she was 25 years old, the age when maintenance and surveys can become prohibitively expensive and a ship is liable to cost more than she can ever be expected to earn. But, surprisingly perhaps, JESSICA carried on in spite of her high fuel consumption and the by-then world-wide greatly increased cost of bunkers. Her Cypriot owners must also have considered her a good investment! The end came in June 1978 when she arrived at her last berth, run ashore at Gadani Beach, Pakistan, to be broken up for scrap. Like her namesake, she ended up being torn apart on a lonely beach far from home: a sad end for what had been a fine and always, as long as I knew her at any rate, a very happy ship.

Somehow, Lamport and Holt colours emphasised the size of ROLAND's funnel.
[Fotoflite incorporating Skyfotos]

Still recognisable as a Lamport and Holt ship, JESSICA on 7th July 1975. Paul Boot, who took the photograph, points out a distinct 'joggle' in her bow, so that the angle of rake between the 20 and 31 feet draft marks is greater than that of the upper and lower bow. This is not apparent in views of DUNEDIN STAR light ship, and may be the result of repairs to collision damage.

THE IMPERIAL STAR CLASS

The IMPERIAL STAR of 1934 and the vessels which followed her over the next 14 years (including the first DUNEDIN STAR) not only gave Blue Star Line a distinctive appearance, but also set superb standards in modern cargo liner design: big cargo carriers, with economical diesels and a comprehensive set of cargo gear. This photographic history of the class illustrates all the ships built to this general design, plus one which never made it into Blue Star ownership. The numbers in brackets after the names refer to the use of that name in the Blue Star fleet, and not just amongst the class.

IMPERIAL STAR (1) (left and below)
Harland & Wolff Ltd., Belfast; 1935, 12,427gt, 524 feet
IMPERIAL STAR, first of the class, is seen left in Gladstone Dock, Liverpool on 10th August 1935, probably at the end of her first round voyage. Apparent in both photographs is the hull band which had been a feature of previous Blue Star ships, but was abandoned sometime in the late 1930s: IMPERIAL STAR was to lose hers around then, and some of the later members of the class never had it.

Large, fast motorships like these were often chosen for Malta convoys, and IMPERIAL STAR was an early victim of one. On 27th September 1941 she was damaged in a raid by Italian aircraft north east of Tunis, fortunately without serious casualties amongst her crew. Although taken in tow by the destroyer HMS ORIBI she became unmanageable and was scuttled the next day.

NEW ZEALAND STAR (1) (opposite top)
Harland & Wolff Ltd., Belfast; 1935, 10,740gt, 524 feet
The first two ships of this group had the boat deck extended forward to the bridge. In all the group, the lack of a mast aft meant that the 'foremast' steaming light had to be attached to the forestay, whilst the 'mainmast' light was just above the crow's nest on the only mast.

In the engine room, this group of ships was not particularly standardised: twin diesels drove twin screws, but there was a considerable difference in the engine specification. IMPERIAL and NEW ZEALAND STARs had 10-cylinder four-strokes designed by Burmeister and Wain, but built by Harland and Wolff.

NEW ZEALAND STAR survived the war, but not the apparently arbitrary transfers of ownership for which Blue Star were notorious. In 1940, together with other members of the class, she was registered under the ownership of Frederick Leyland and Co. Ltd. In 1950 owners became Lamport and Holt Line Ltd., and 1953 the Booth Steamship Co. Ltd. None of the post-war changes affected the funnel colours, which remained those of Blue Star until she was broken up at Kure, Japan in August 1967.

AUSTRALIA STAR (1) (above and right)
Harland & Wolff Ltd., Belfast; 1935, 11,122gt, 524 feet
AUSTRALIA STAR marked a change to 6-cylinder two-stroke engines, again of Danish design, and this installation was used for the next five Harland & Wolff ships. They also differed from the IMPERIAL and NEW ZEALAND STARs in having a raised poop.

For a period during the sixties, AUSTRALIA STAR had a lilac-coloured hull, her crew becoming known as the 'Lavender Hull Mob'. Later, she became grey, possibly because lilac was too close to Union Castle's hull colour.

The lower view shows AUSTRALIA STAR leaving Liverpool in June 1964 for Faslane to be demolished by Shipbreaking Industries Ltd. The flags celebrated both the Queen's Official Birthday and the last voyage of a gallant ship.

EMPIRE STAR (2)
Harland & Wolff Ltd., Belfast; 1935, 11,093gt, 524 feet

The name EMPIRE STAR probably reflected the title 'Empire Food Ships' given to the refrigerated cargo liners built in some numbers in the 1930s. It was certainly not a fortunate one for the ship, which was attacked twice during 1942 with heavy loss of life. On 12th February, EMPIRE STAR was helping in the evacuation of Singapore when seriously damaged by Japanese aircraft in the Durian Strait. There were 16 casualties, and EMPIRE STAR needed extensive repairs in Australia. She was even less fortunate on what was probably her next outward voyage. En route from Liverpool to South Africa she was sunk by the German submarine U 615 north of the Azores. This time, 32 crew, gunners and passengers were lost.

DUNEDIN STAR (1)
Cammell, Laird and Co. Ltd., Birkenhead; 1936, 11,168gt, 530 feet

Despite their lack of conventional masts aft of the superstructure, these ships yet had a grace of hull form, which can be appreciated in this three-quarter stern view. The first of several Birkenhead-built members of the class, DUNEDIN STAR also pioneered 9-cylinder two-stroke Swiss-built Sulzer diesels. The story of her wartime loss, through marine hazard rather than enemy action, is told in Captain Kinghorn's article (see page 17).

SYDNEY STAR
Harland & Wolff Ltd., Belfast; 1936, 11,095gt, 524 feet
SYDNEY STAR survived at least one Malta convoy, although on her arrival in Valletta on 24th July 1941 damage inflicted by a German E-boat necessitated dry-docking before she could leave.

Sold to a Greek company in 1967 for her final voyage east, SYDNEY STAR was named KENT: rather a cheeky gesture, as this was suggestive of rival Federal Line's nomenclature! The final voyage ended at Taiwan on 11th August 1967.

MELBOURNE STAR (1)
Cammell, Laird and Co. Ltd., Birkenhead; 1936, 11,076gt, 530 feet
The fourth type of engine, a 10-cylinder Sulzer model, was introduced with the MELBOURNE STAR.

Of the five ships of this class sunk by enemy action during the war, the MELBOURNE STAR was to be the most grievous loss. She had her first taste of action in September 1940 when attacked by German aircraft off Ireland, but was repaired and returned to the fray. On 2nd June 1943 she was torpedoed by the German submarine U 129 south east of Bermuda whilst on a voyage from the UK to Australia via Panama with a cargo including ammunition and torpedoes. She had on board a mammoth complement of 117 crew, gunners and passengers, of whom only four survived.

BRISBANE STAR (1)
Cammell, Laird and Co. Ltd., Birkenhead; 1937, 11,076gt, 530 feet

The exploits of BRISBANE STAR in a Malta convoy in August 1942 were discussed in *Record* 8, which also showed the bow damage inflicted by an airborne torpedo. This damage saw her run with an imitation of a Meierform bow until permanent repairs could be carried out. Her postwar service was, in contrast, dull: a nominal transfer to Lamport and Holt Line Ltd. between 1950 and 1959 being outwardly unrecorded. In July 1963 came the shock of transfer to the Liberian flag as ENEA, but this was for just one voyage east, which ended at a breakers' yard at Osaka on 15th October 1963.

WELLINGTON STAR (1)
Harland & Wolff Ltd., Belfast; 1939, 12,382gt, 536 feet

Although a few feet longer than her forerunners, WELLINGTON STAR was clearly built to the same design. She is seen running trials: probably the last time she appeared in full Blue Star colours, as her completion in September 1939 coincided with the outbreak of war. Her service was to be tragically short. On 16th June 1940 she was west of Cape Finisterre, homeward bound from Australia with a general cargo, when torpedoed by the German submarine U 101. She was, presumably, in convoy as her entire complement of 69 was rescued. *[Ulster Folk and Transport Museum, 4325]*

AUCKLAND STAR (1) (top and middle)
Harland & Wolff Ltd., Belfast; 1939, 12,382gt, 536 feet
AUCKLAND STAR is launched at Belfast on 20th June 1939. Her career was even briefer than that of WELLINGTON STAR, and such was the protracted nature of wartime voyages that she did not even complete a round trip. On 28th July 1940 she was heading for Liverpool from Townsville with almost 11,000 tons of cargo which was of utmost value to the war effort – lead, steel, wheat, and refrigerated food – when torpedoed by Otto Kretschmer's U 99 off Cape Clear, Ireland. Fortunately, as in the case of WELLINGTON STAR, there were no fatalities amongst her crew of 74. She is seen at Auckland in the middle photograph.
[Top: Ulster Folk and Transport Museum; Middle: W. Laxon collection]

DZIERZYNSKI ex ADELAIDE STAR (1) (bottom)
Akt. Burmeister & Wain's Maskin & Skibsbyggerri, Copenhagen, Denmark; 1943, 12,636gt, 528 feet
This ship was so clearly intended to be a member of the class that she deserves a place in this story. Blue Star never operated her, although they certainly paid for most of her. Her Danish builders launched her as ADELAIDE STAR in December 1939, but she was seized by the Germans on their invasion in April 1940, completed as SEEBURG in 1943 and operated by HAPAG as a submarine depot ship, or a target ship (she was probably used in both roles). During the great evacuation from the east she was sunk in the Gulf of Danzig on 2nd December 1944 by the Russian submarine SC 407, although a minefield laid by the RAF and dubbed 'Spinach 1' has also been credited. But this was not the end of her story: Polish salvors raised the wreck in 1951 (1954 according to one account) and after protracted repairs at Gdynia she joined the fleet of Polish Ocean Lines in 1957 as DZIERZYNSKI. It is doubtful whether the new owners really had their value from her, as in September 1963 she became involved in a series of accidents. On the 19th September she was off Ushant during a voyage from Shanghai to Gdynia when involved in a collision in fog with the FOULI (692/1948, but better known as the Monks' steam coaster SPRAYVILLE which

had just been sold to Greek owners). Although damage was not serious, DZIERZYNSKI put into the Scheldt, where the situation quickly deteriorated. Near Antwerp's Baudouin Lock she collided with a pier with such force that she had to be beached to prevent sinking. Unfortunately, she broke in two and was fit for nothing but scrap. Her remarkable career had spanned 23 years, but a significant proportion of it

EMPIRE STAR (3) (top)
Harland & Wolff Ltd., Belfast; 1946, 11,861gt, 521 feet

The later EMPIRE STAR was the odd one out of this group, being launched for the Ministry of Transport as EMPIRE MERCIA, and joining Blue Star on her completion in December 1946. Almost identical were Port Line's PORT HOBART (11,877/1946) ex-EMPIRE WESSEX and Shaw Savill's WAIWERA (12,028/1944). EMPIRE STAR can be distinguished from the other 13 ships of the group by an extended bridge deck and a raised poop.

EMPIRE STAR along with the two final Blue Star ships of the class was fitted with yet another type of engine: an 8-cylinder two-stroke, again built under licence from Burmeister & Wain. Her career was relatively mundane: completed for Frederick Leyland and Co. Ltd., she was formally transferred to Lamport and Holt Line Ltd. in 1950 with no change of name or colours. The delightfully-named Long John Industrial Co. Ltd. bought her in 1971 and took her to Kaohsiung for demolition.

IMPERIAL STAR (2) (middle)
Harland & Wolff Ltd., Belfast; 1948, 13,181gt, 550 feet

The two post-war completions were distinguished by elegant curved plate stems, all the previous vessels having straight bar stems.

Blue Star had maximum service from this group of ships - at least, from those that survived the war. They were spared the indignity of peeling paint and minimal maintenance whilst voyaging under some dubious flag, even though several were sold right at the end of their careers this was usually for just one voyage to the breakers. The second IMPERIAL STAR was spared even this passing indignity, and is recorded as arriving at Kaohsiung on 17th September 1971 under her original name.

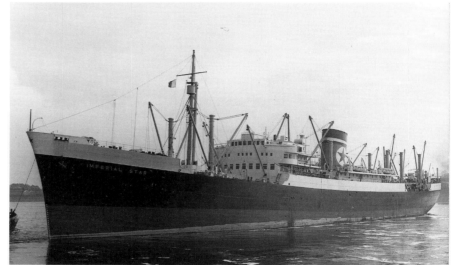

MELBOURNE STAR (2) (bottom)
Harland & Wolff Ltd., Belfast; 1948, 13,179gt, 550 feet

MELBOURNE STAR was the last of the class to be built – 13 years after the first – and, by a narrow margin, the last to survive. In May 1972 she was sold for service as a floating cold store at Piraeus. Later that summer she sailed east under the Greek flag with her name contracted to MELBO, but – although she was handed over to the Tung Cheng Steel and Iron Works in August 1972 – work was not begun until early 1973 and officially completed on 7th April that year.

GILLISON AND CHADWICK'S 'DRUM LINE' SAILING SHIPS
John Naylon

This list of vessels owned by James Gillison and Joseph Chadwick is a follow up to *'Omega – the last of her race',* which appeared in *Record* 8. Besides the unique record of the DRUMCLIFF/ OMEGA, there were some other units of the 'Drum' fleet which contributed in one way or another to the saga of sail.

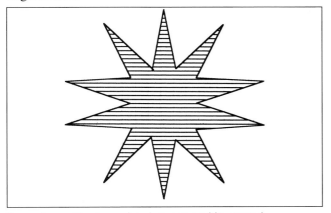

House flag: a blue ten-pointed star on a white ground
[J.L. Loughran]

BRITISH ARMY: the dangers of petroleum cargoes

In January 1896 the BRITISH ARMY was lying at Barry Dock, having carried a cargo of naphtha from New York to Blaye, near Bordeaux, and then pit props to Barry. On the 28th of the month the vessel was being swept out by Messrs. Lloyd and White, contractors, while marine store dealers were searching the bilges, with the aid of a candle, for salvable coconut oil from a previous cargo. An explosion of naphtha vapour killed a man and a boy and severely injured five others. The subsequent inquiry by Colonel Sir Vivian Dering Majendie, KCB, Her Majesty's Chief Inspector of Explosives, cited nine other vessels which had been lost or seriously damaged by vapour explosions, the risk being highest in empty ships. Sir Vivian emphasized the need for careful cleansing of the holds of vessels which had carried petroleum and urged the Board of Trade to make general regulations about carriage and ventilation.

The finger of fate was obviously pointing at the BRITISH ARMY in 1896. Her career ended six months later when she was dismasted on passage Barry to Pisagua with coal.

DRUMELTAN: salved by the Royal Navy

The DRUMELTAN's service with Gillison and Chadwick ended in 1894 when on 25th April, on passage from Shanghai to Tacoma in ballast, under Captain T.E. Cowell and with a crew of thirty, she stranded on the south end of Tanega-Shima Island,

Japan. She was salved two months later by the six vessels of the British China Squadron under Captain Fawkes. Lieutenant Tuppen, in charge of the working parties, took 17 days to lighten her and haul her bows round to seaward, when she was refloated by HMS SEVERN and towed to Nagasaki. Abandoned by the underwriters as a constructive total loss, she was sold in 1896 to S.C. Farnham and Co. of Shanghai, but soon stranded again on Saddle Island, 80 miles south east of that port. This time she was salvaged by the Shanghai Dock Co., towed back to Shanghai, repaired, re-rigged and in 1898 sold to F. E. Bliss of London. In 1899 she sailed from Shanghai to New York – the only Chinese-flag sailing vessel ever to enter the Hudson – and on arrival was acquired by the Anglo American Oil Co. Ltd. of London, beginning a career of 20 years in the case oil (kerosene) trade to the Far East.

DRUMMUIR: a part in the battle of the Falklands

The DRUMMUIR had a dramatic end. One of the most exciting naval operations of the First World War was the dash by two battle cruisers, HMS INVINCIBLE and INFLEXIBLE, from the North Sea to the Falkland Islands, some 7,000 miles, to seek out and destroy the German squadron under Vice-Admiral Graf von Spee which shortly before had sunk HMS GOOD HOPE and MONMOUTH, with Admiral Craddock and all hands, off Coronel on the west coast of South America.

On 2nd December 1914 the DRUMMUIR was captured 30 miles south west of Staten Island by the German cruiser SMS LEIPZIG while bound from Port Talbot to Caleta Coloso with 2,750 tons of anthracite. LEIPZIG, together with SCHARNHORST, NÜRNBERG, GNEISENAU and DRESDEN, was bound east to attack the Falklands after the victory at Coronel five weeks earlier. The DRUMMUIR was taken to Picton Island and her cargo transferred to the colliers BADEN and ISABELLA, after which she was sunk by explosive charges at 3.00pm on 6th December, six miles offshore in position 55.30 south by 65.00 west – despite protestations that she was United States-owned though under the British flag. However, the four-day delay by the Germans in unloading the DRUMMUIR allowed Admiral Sturdee's British squadron to arrive first at the Falklands, where he defeated von Spee two days after the sinking of the DRUMMUIR.

The lofty DRUMROCK

Although we customarily associate skysails with the British and American clippers of the tea, wool and California trades, a surprising number of the big carriers of the 'nineties sported these fancy kites. None was more impressive than the three-skysail-yarder DRUMROCK, described by Lubbock as 'one of the finest examples of Ramage and Ferguson's work. Besides being an excellent sailer she was most beautifully finished and elaborately fitted'.

Commanded by Captain T.S. Bailey throughout her career under the red ensign, she put up some good performances; for instance, 5 days, 6 hours and 15 minutes from San Francisco to Tacoma in November 1894, and 85 days from Liverpool to Calcutta in 1897. When Laiesz bought her in 1899 and renamed her PERSIMMON, they installed brace and halliard winches and put her into the west coast of South America nitrate trade, where she kept up the high standards of the company by making excellent passages, for instance: 1899 Lizard-Taltal 74 days and Iquique-Lizard 78 days; 1900 Dungeness-Taltal 76 days; 1901 Lizard-Valparaiso 70 days and Iquique-Lizard 86 days; 1903 Dungeness-Valparaiso 75 days and Iquique-Scilly 80 days; 1904 Lizard-Valparaiso 74 days; and 1910 Lizard-Valparaiso 72 days. The 1910 passage, under Captain Oetzmann, was marked by tragedy. In May and June, while off Cape Horn, the PERSIMMON lost eight of her crew – three in falls from aloft and five in the upending of a lifeboat in a rescue attempt.

After Vinnens of Bremen bought her in 1913 and renamed her, the HELWIG VINNEN only made one complete voyage for her new owners, to Mejillones and back, early in 1914. Leaving Hamburg again on 21st April 1914 with coke for the Santa Rosalía smelter, she arrived at the Mexican port in 132 days, on the last day of the fateful month of August. After discharging, Captain Herman Wessel had a charter to load grain in the Pacific North West; but in fact he and his ship remained in Santa Rosalía for nine years – by which time only three of the original crew of 28 were left.

In 1920 the HELWIG VINNEN was allocated to France as war reparations, but France was on the point of winding-up its subsidized sailing fleet and the vessel was not taken up. In 1921 she was bought, along with the other German sailing ships detained at Santa Rosalía, by Robert Dollar of San Francisco, with a view to employment in the lumber trade from the Pacific North West to the Orient. Dollar intended to rename the vessel ALLEN DOLLAR, but that name was never officially used and she never sailed under it. The HELWIG VINNEN finally left Santa Rosalía in tow on 23rd November 1923, but instead of resuming a trading life she was put on the mud at Alameda Island, San Francisco Bay.

From 1924 to 1927 she returned to a kind of life as a cut-down log barge, passing through three Vancouver owners, the last of whom, the Pacific Coyle Navigation Co., restored her original name. Finally, in this harsh trade, on 1st February 1927 she stranded on rocks in Takuish Harbour, Smith's Inlet, Queen Charlotte Sound, while carrying logs from Masset, Queen Charlotte Island, to Mainland Mills, Powell River, in tow of the tug PACIFIC MONARCH. The Pacific Salvage Company's steamer SALVAGE KING was despatched from Victoria to refloat her but the DRUMROCK had broken her back.

List of 'Drum Line' sailing ships

1. DRUMLANRIG 1876-1900 Iron ship
O.N. 74556   Signal letters QJKV   1,482g 1,425n   241.5 x 37.7 x 22.6 feet
23.8.1876: Launched by Russell and Co., Port Glasgow (Yard No. 7) for Gillison and Chadwick, Liverpool as DRUMLANRIG.
20.2.1899: Put into Montevideo for repairs after partial dismasting whilst on passage Liverpool to Victoria, British Columbia.
1900: Sold to Flli. Repetto fu G.B. (Repetto Brothers), Genoa, Italy and renamed GIO. BATTA REPETTO.
2.10.1905: Sunk in collision with the French steamer MATAPAN (3,613/1884) off Ibiza whilst on a voyage from Liverpool to Genoa with a cargo of coal. Four of her crew were lost. Blame for the accident was attached to MATAPAN.

2. DRUMPARK 1877-1897 Iron ship
O.N. 76529   Signal letters QWBS   1,551g 1,470n   243.6 x 37.9 x 22.6 feet
7.1877: Launched by W.H. Potter and Son, Liverpool (Yard No. 73) for Gillison and Chadwick, Liverpool as DRUMPARK.
1897: Sold to Flli. G.B. and G. Figari di F., Genoa, Italy
1911: Broken up at Genoa.

3. CALLIXENE 1878-1884 Wooden ship
O.N. 63208   Signal letters KSMJ   1,369g 1,337n   195.2 x 38.5 x 24.1 feet
1869: Completed by Nevins, Courtenay Bay, St. John, New Brunswick for William and Richard Wright, Liverpool as CALLIXENE.
1878: Acquired by Gillison and Chadwick, Liverpool.
1884: Sold to John R. Suiter, Maryport.
1893: Sold for use as coal hulk at Gibraltar.

4. BRITISH SOVEREIGN 1880-1881 Iron ship
O.N. 51030   Signal letters WLNV   1,345g 1,292n   213.2 x 34.2 x 22.8 feet
10.1864: Launched by Robinson, Cork for the British Shipowners Co. Ltd., Liverpool as BRITISH SOVEREIGN.
1880: Acquired by Gillison and Chadwick, Liverpool.
24.4.1881: Sailed from Dundee for San Francisco with coal, with crew of 23 under Captain W. Gillison, and went missing.

5. DRUMBURTON 1881-1900 Four-masted iron ship
O.N. 84131   Signal letters WKVP   1,891g 1,773n   266.7 x 40.2 x 23.9 feet
15.7.1881: Launched by Russell and Co., Port Glasgow (Yard No. 36) for Gillison and Chadwick, Liverpool as DRUMBURTON.
1900: Sold to Ship Drumburton Co. Ltd. (Western Commercial Co.), Victoria, British Columbia.
7.11.1903: Explosion of coal gas in position 20.00 north by 124.00 east whilst on passage from Manila to San Francisco in ballast. One man was killed.
3.9.1904: Went ashore in dense fog and broke up near Cliff House, Point San Pedro, 10 miles north of San Francisco, whilst on passage from San Francisco to Port Blakely, Puget Sound, in ballast. Crew of 24 under Captain W. Thomas.

The iron full rigger DRUMLANRIG initiated the 'Drum' nomenclature in the Gillison and Chadwick fleet (opposite). Although built only seven years later than the CALLIXENE, and of similar tonnage, she vividly illustrates the diverging shipbuilding practices of Britain and North America. *[San Francisco Maritime National Historical Park]*

The big wooden barque, ex-full rigger, CALLIXENE (above) was an oddity in the Gillison and Chadwick fleet. Her first owners were William and Richard Wright, formerly shipbuilders of St. John, New Brunswick. They moved to Liverpool in 1855 and were in business there until the late 1880s, but continued to place orders in St. John yards. By 1876 they had ten New Brunswick-built vessels registered in

Liverpool. Although here reduced to barque rig, the CALLIXENE still carries the mizzen mast of a full rigger. She is unmistakably a North American-built wooden ship with her outside channels, full-length figurehead on an upright stem, and a heavy squared-off poop, where an officer poses for the photograph while another figure stands on top of the charthouse. *[Author's collection]*

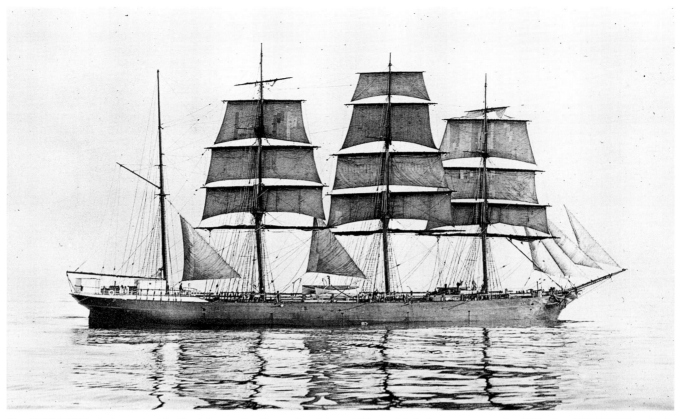

The DRUMMUIR photographed by Captain Orison E. Beaton in Puget Sound, Washington, on 26th February 1913, when she was owned in Victoria, B.C. The wheelhouse is a later addition, added after she was sold to Canada in 1900. Boards have been fitted above the main rail for carrying a timber deck load. On her maiden voyage in 1882 the DRUMMUIR, which originally carried a main skysail, went out to Melbourne in 88 days. [San Francisco Maritime National Historical Park]

6. BRITISH ARMY 1882-1896 Iron barque
O.N. 62332   Signal letters WPTV   1,338g 1,289n   221.1 x 36.9 x 22.6 feet
9.1869: Launched by T.R. Oswald, Sunderland (Yard No. 83) for Middle Dock Co., Sunderland as the iron ship CYNRIC.
1872: Sold to British Shipowners Co. Ltd., Liverpool and renamed BRITISH ARMY.
1880: Converted to a barque.
1882: Acquired by Gillison and Chadwick, Liverpool.
28.1.1896: Explosion of naphtha vapour in the hold, while lying at Barry Dock. Two killed and five seriously injured.
6.6.1896: Dismasted in west south west gale, force 8, in the South Atlantic in position 54.30 south by 62.00 west whilst on passage from Barry to Pisagua with coal. One man lost. Put back to Rio de Janeiro, where she was condemned and hulked. Later reported as hulk at Valparaiso.

7. DRUMMUIR 1882-1899 Iron four-masted barque
O.N. 86233   Signal letters JBFS   1,844g 1,798n   270.5 x 39.2 x 24.0 feet
8.1882: Launched by W.H. Potter and Son, Liverpool (Yard No. 106) for Gillison and Chadwick, Liverpool as DRUMMUIR.
1899: Sold to F.W. Webster, Liverpool.
1900: Sold to Ship Drummuir Co. Ltd. (Western Commercial Co., managers), Victoria, British Columbia.
1905: Sold to Captain John Barneson (Barneson-Hibberd Co., managers), Victoria.
1914: Sold to Hind, Rolph Co., Victoria (James Rolph, San Francisco, manager).
2.12.1914: Captured by the German cruiser SMS LEIPZIG thirty miles south west of Staten Island, Argentina.
6.12.1914: Sunk by explosive charges in position 55.30 south by 65.00 west.

8. DRUMBLAIR 1883-1905 Iron four-masted barque
O.N. 87900   Signal letters JBFM   1,907g 1,848n   267.4 x 40.2 x 24.1 feet
4.9.1883: Launched by Russell and Co., Greenock (Yard No.80) for Gillison and Chadwick, Liverpool as DRUMBLAIR.
16.9.1892: Stranded two and a half miles west of Shallow Inlet, Waratah Bay, Victoria, Australia. Captain William Goulding was censured by the Court of Inquiry for careless navigation, disregarding compass errors and gross misconduct; and his certificate was suspended for 3 months.
1905: Sold to William Bowen, Llanelly and renamed CISSIE.
1912: Sold to Bech and Co., Tvedestrand, Norway.
1914: Sold to E. Monsen and Co., Tvedestrand.
21.10.1915: Sunk in collision with the steamer NORTHWESTERN MILLER (5,046/1915), 13 miles south by east of the Nab Light Vessel off the Isle of Wight whilst on passage from Hull to Gulfport in ballast, to be hulked. Seven of her crew of 22 were lost.

9. DRUMELTAN 1883-1894 Iron four-masted barque
O.N. 87920   Signal letters JCQH   1,908g 1,820n   267.3 x 40.3 x 24.1 feet
19.11.1883: Launched by Russell and Co., Greenock (Yard No. 88) for Gillison and Chadwick, Liverpool as DRUMELTAN.
25.4.1894: Stranded on Tanega-Shima Island, Japan, whilst on passage from Shanghai to Tacoma. Refloated by British China Squadron and towed to Nagasaki.
1896: Sold to S.C. Farnham and Co., Shanghai. Stranded on Saddle Island, 80 miles south east of Shanghai. Salvaged by Shanghai Dock Co., towed back to Shanghai, repaired and re-rigged.
1898: Sold to Drumeltan Sailing Ship Co. Ltd. (F.E. Bliss, manager), London.
1899: Sold to Anglo American Oil Co. Ltd., London.

The DRUMBLAIR (above), Captain H. Davies, in Commencement Bay, Washington, 1899, in a typical portrait by Wilhelm Hester of Seattle. The early 1880s were evidently the period of transition in headgear from the old-fashioned bowsprit and jibboom to the spike bowsprit. The sister ships DRUMBLAIR and DRUMELTAN (1883) carry the old arrangement while the DRUMMUIR (1882) already sports the new spar. *[San Francisco Maritime National Historical Park]*

The CISSIE (ex-DRUMBLAIR) at Cape Town, making repairs to her foremast (right). The topgallantmast and all the yards except the foreyard have been sent down, and the jibboom has been run in. *[Author's collection]*

H.N. Cooper of Seacombe took this photograph of the DRUMELTAN lying in the Mersey when she was owned by the Standard Oil Company. Her royal yards have been sent down for a ballast passage. The DRUMELTAN was one of the oldest and smallest units of Standard Oil's fleet of 23 sailing vessels, but she nevertheless served one or other of the company's subsidiaries from 1899 to 1921.

1912: Transferred to Tank Storage and Carriage Co. Ltd., Hong Kong.

1916: Transferred to Standard Transportation Co., Hong Kong.

1921: Sold to Browne and Willis, New York, U.S.A. but registered at Punta Arenas, Costa Rica, and renamed MARGARET OVERMAN.

1922: Sold to Neptune Lines Inc., New York, converted to schooner and renamed BROOKLYN.

1930: Sold to Durham Navigation Co., New York.

1931: Sold to A. and S. Transportation Co., Newark, New Jersey, U.S.A. and converted to schooner barge. Later sold to Merritt, Chapman and Scott Corporation, New York, as sewage barge.

2.6.1936: Run down and sunk by oil barge NEWARK off New York while in tow of the CHAPMAN BROTHERS (472/1915).

10. TYTHONUS 1884-1897 Iron barque
O.N. 44702 Signal letters TWGC 1,152g 1,152n 201.0 x 36.0 x 22.9 feet

7.1862: Launched by Pile, Spence and Co., West Hartlepool (Yard No. 423) for J. Smurthwaite, Sunderland as the iron ship TYTHONUS.

1865: Sold to Stuart and Douglas, Liverpool.

1877: Rerigged as barque.

1884: Acquired by Gillison and Chadwick, Liverpool.

1897: Sold to Aktieselskabet Tythonus (Harold Haslum, manager), Moss, Norway.

1899: Manager became B.J. Grefstad, Grimstad, Norway.

19.10.1901: Burnt in the South Atlantic whilst on a voyage from Fleetwood to Valparaiso with a cargo of coal.

11. DRUMCRAIG 1885-1902 Iron four-masted barque
O.N. 91178 Signal letters JTGP 1,970g 1,919n 280.4 x 41.1 x 23.5 feet

19.1.1885: Launched by the Barrow Shipbuilding Co., Barrow-in-Furness (Yard No. 128) for Gillison and Chadwick, Liverpool as DRUMCRAIG.

1898-1899: Made a protracted passage of 173 days from Swansea to San Francisco, having lost her main topmast off the Brazilian coast and making the rest of the passage under jury rig via the Cape of Good Hope.

1902: Sold to Western Commercial Co., Victoria, British Columbia.

1905: Sold to Captain John Barneson, Victoria.

20.9.1905: Left Astoria on passage from Portland, Oregon to Manila with lumber.

19.3.1906: Bottle found containing message 'Ship sinking 43 degrees north/127 degrees west'.

18.4.1906: Posted missing.

12. DRUMCLIFF 1887-1898 Iron four-masted barque
O.N. 93713 Signal letters KJVQ 2,468g 2,525n 311.3
x 43.2 x 24.2 feet

14.1.1887: Launched by Russell and Co., Greenock (Yard
No. 160) for Gillison and Chadwick, Liverpool as
DRUMCLIFF.

20.7.1898: Sold to Rhederei-Aktien-Gesellschaft von
1896, Hamburg, Germany and renamed OMEGA.

1914-1919: Interned at Callao, Peru.

1919: Allocated as war reparations to Peru and became
schoolship.

1926: Passed to Compañía Administradora del Guano,
Lima, Peru.

26.6.1958: Foundered whilst on passage from the
Pachacamac Islands to Huacho.

13. DRUMROCK 1891-1899 Steel four-masted barque
O.N. 99316 Signal letters MHGP 3,182g 3,010n 329.2
x 45.4 x 25.7 feet

5.8.1891: Launched by Ramage and Ferguson, Leith (Yard
No. 108) for Gillison and Chadwick, Liverpool as
DRUMROCK.

1899: Sold to Rhederei F. Laiesz, Hamburg, Germany and
renamed PERSIMMON.

4.1913: Sold to F.A. Vinnen und Söhne (Bremer Stahlhof
A.G.), Bremen, Germany and renamed HELWIG
VINNEN.

1914-1918: Interned at Santa Rosalía, Mexico.

1920: Allocated to France as war reparations but not taken
up.

1921: Sold to Robert Dollar and Co., San Francisco,
U.S.A. and renamed ALLEN DOLLAR. Laid up Oakland
Creek.

1924: Sold to Hecate Straits Towing Co., Vancouver,
British Columbia for use as a log barge and renamed LOG
TYEE.

1926: Sold to B.L. Johnson, Walton and Co., Vancouver.

1.2.1927: Strandard and broke up in Takuish Harbour,
Smith's Inlet, Queen Charlotte Sound, while in tow of tug
PACIFIC MONARCH (286/1912).

The DRUMCRAIG off Cape Flattery or in the Strait of Juan de Fuca, photographed from her tug by Hiram Hudson Morrison (above right). Captain Morrison, along with fellow tugboat masters Orison E. Beaton and George E. Plummer, took many fine sailing-ship photos in the Strait of Juan de Fuca or at the entrance to the Columbia River. The DRUMCRAIG of 1885 carries the new spike bowsprit, unlike the old bowsprit and jibboom of her stablemates of two years earlier. *[San Francisco Maritime National Historical Park]*

The HELWIG VINNEN (ex-PERSIMMON, ex-DRUMROCK) interned at Santa Rosalía, Mexico, during the First World War (left). As the PERSIMMON, she was the only Laiesz Flying-P Line vessel to carry skysails. When Vinnens bought her in 1913 they removed the mizzen skysail and pole, and here the fore and main skysail yards have also been sent down. The jigger mast has been fitted with typical German double gaffs. *[Jürgen Meyer collection]*

'... undoubtedly one of the finest steel sailing ships ever built' (Basil Lubbock). The three-skysail-yarder DRUMROCK, Captain T.S. Bailey, lies ready for sea in Commencement Bay, Washington, 1894. At this date she was the largest sailing vessel ever seen in Puget Sound and she lies loaded with a record cargo of 5,000 tons of wheat from Tacoma. The double steering wheel was unusual in British sailing ships and the long jib-headed spanker was much more common on American vessels. [Wilhelm Hester Collection, San Francisco Maritime National Historical Park]

BOWATERS REVISITED

Since the feature on Bowaters' ships in *Record* 5, some particularly interesting photographs have turned up. We thank Captain Hubert Hall, of Yarmouth, Nova Scotia for photographs and notes on LIVERPOOL ROVER, and Tony Smith of the World Ship Photo Library who kindly loaned us photographs recently acquired by the Society.

Thanks also to Bill Laxon, who adds another short-lived Bowater's ship to our list, the R.J. CULLEN (6,693/1917). Built by the Osaka Iron Works Ltd. as the EASTERN KNIGHT, she was later SAN LUCAS, in 1940 being registered in St. John, New Brunswick as R.J. CULLEN for the Atlantic Transportation Co. This company was managed by the Bowater-owned International Paper and Power Co. R.J. CULLEN was wrecked two miles north of Leinish, Castlebay, Barra on 15th January 1942 whilst on ballast passage from Liverpool (the English one) to Sydney (the one in Nova Scotia).

LIVERPOOL ROVER (1)

John I. Thornycroft & Co. Ltd., Southampton; 1920, 1,426gt, 240 feet

The Mersey Paper Company's LIVERPOOL ROVER is shown in the St. Peters Canal at St. Peters, Cape Breton, Nova Scotia. Her deckload of hand-stowed pulpwood from the Bras d'Or Lakes of Nova Scotia would be destined for the company's mill at Brooklyn, Nova Scotia.

Captain Hubert Hall recalls that, in the late 1950s he was on the pulpwood run to Brooklyn, Nova Scotia on her successor, LIVERPOOL ROVER (2) ex MARKLAND, built in 1929. Then the pulpwood was loaded from a floating conveyor which dumped it directly into the holds, unstowed. At Brooklyn it was discharged by four finger-grabs. Hubert was on this ship when Bowater's took over the company and, as a seaman, was involved in changing the colours from the Markland Shipping Company to Bowater's cream-and-green scheme (shown on page 10 of *Record* 6). Somehow, he felt, the new colours just did not seem to enhance this relatively old and rather ungainly ship. The original colours were black hull, buff bulwarks and funnel, and white superstructure.

The LIVERPOOL ROVER illustrated was built by a company better known for their naval work than their merchant ships, but who would need alternative employment in the lean years immediately after the First World War. Initial owners were French, for whom she sailed as VILLE DE SAINT AMARIN, but in 1922 she was bought by Cardiff owners, F.E. & O.T. Lewis and Co. Ltd., who registered her under the Tudor Steam Navigation Co. Ltd. as TUDOR KING. In 1933 she was renamed LIVERPOOL ROVER by a company giving itself the unwieldy name the Schooner Trawler Fishing Co. Ltd. of Liverpool, Nova Scotia. Quite what this company attempted to do is unclear, but it had links with the Markland Shipping Co. Ltd. (itself a subsidiary of the Mersey Paper Company), and within a year LIVERPOOL ROVER was transferred to the more conventionally-named Rover Shipping Co. Ltd. She ran in the wood pulp trade until June 1946 when sold to Wheelock, Marden and Co. Ltd. who renamed her ROVERLOCK. This Shanghai company was attempting to

rebuild its shipping interests, and actually bought a large number of Flower class corvettes for conversion to cargo ships. However, post-war Shanghai was not a stable place to rebuild a business, and most of the acquired ships were soon sold, ROVERLOCK becoming the AN LIEN for another Shanghai owner. She, and presumably the owner, fled to Taipeh in the face of the communists, and AN LIEN was broken up in 1953. *[Both: Hubert Hall collection]*

SANDLAND

Swan, Hunter and Wigham Richardson Ltd., Newcastle-upon-Tyne; 1925, 2,213gt, 251 feet

Easily the most exciting of the WSPL photographs was this example of necessity being the mother of invention. SANDLAND had begun life as a sand-pump dredger, built for service on the St. Lawrence and Great Lakes, as were so many Swan, Hunter products of the period (an article on Swan's canallers is due for publication in *Record*). In 1943 a shipyard at Port Dalhousie lengthened her and converted her to a freighter for Bowater's Newfoundland Pulp and Paper Mills Ltd., who used her in Canadian waters and traded her down to the United States. In 1948, with the urgent need for tonnage over, SANDLAND was sold to Montreal. She passed through the hands of a number of owners, retaining her 1925 name. Her original MacColl and Pollock triple-expansion engine was taken out in 1953 and replaced with a Canadian-built diesel which was itself already 11 years old. After 38 years in Canadian waters, SANDLAND went to Venezuelan owners in 1963 to become TRITON, receiving another 1942-built diesel in 1967. She was deleted from *Lloyd's Registers* in 1974 after being broken up – almost fifty years and three engines after being built on the Tyne.

NORTH BROOK (middle)

McDougall-Duluth Co., Duluth, Minnesota; 1919, 2,373gt, 251 feet

NORTHBROOK was illustrated in wartime in both *Record* 5 and the follow-up on page 128 of *Record* 6, yet this shot tells another story, of operating in the frozen waters around Corner Brook, Newfoundland. This was a ship which was not built for the trade, but was a simple and modest-sized war-standard freighter.

KITTY'S BROOK (bottom)

Irvine's Shipbuilding & Drydock Co. Ltd., West Hartlepool; 1907, 4,031gt, 325 feet

This photograph is probably unique. KITTY'S BROOK was acquired in 1941, but

was torpedoed and sunk by the German submarine U 588 off the US east coast in position 42.56 north by 63.59 west on 10th May 1942 whilst carrying United States Government stores from New York to Argentia, Newfoundland. Nine lives were lost, but vengeance was swift, and the U-boat was itself sunk by a Canadian corvette that July.

KITTY'S BROOK had been built as Elder, Dempster's ABONEMA, one of three sisters.

In 1920 a change of heart, or perhaps change of trade, saw her becoming SAPELE for the same owners. When sold in 1929, the first of three Argentinean owners bought her, renaming her SAN GEORGE and converting her Richardsons, Westgarth triple-expansion engines to oil burning. In 1935 she became SANTA CATHARINA, as which Bowater's Newfoundland Pulp and Paper Mills Ltd. probably paid a high price for a ship which gave them barely a year's work. *[All: World Ship Photo Library]*

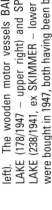

Bowaters used several tugs at Corner Brook. PREVENTOR (317/1929) was built at Montreal for the Minister of National Revenue, Ottawa which suggests she was a patrol or customs vessel - and is seen top left in wartime grey on

United States yards, at Rockville, Maine and Jacksonville, Florida, respectively, presumably for the US military. [All: World Ship Photo Library]

The wooden motor vessels BALSAM LAKE (178/1947 – upper right) and SPRUCE LAKE (238/1941, ex SKIMMER – lower right) were bought in 1947, both having been built in

18th May 1942. Bowater's Newfoundland Pulp and Paper Mills Ltd. acquired the little motor ship during the Second World War, and she is seen in their ownership in 1946 (lower

TWO-FUNNEL CARGO LINERS
Part Three

Readers have responded superbly to our call for names and photographs of two-funnel cargo liners additional to those we listed and illustrated in *Records* 7 and 8, and we are able to illustrate several more of this type including a couple of cargo ships from the far east which come within our remit. We also include follow-up in the way of letters about and photographs of ships mentioned in the earlier articles in this series.

ST. RONANS
Earle's Shipbuilding and Engineering Co. Ltd., Hull; 1881, 4,484gt, 402 feet
Taken in her original homeport of Liverpool, this photograph shows the ST. RONANS with Mersey steam flats alongside. Original owners were Rankin, Gilmour and Co., but whether this is their funnel colours is open to doubt, as they used red, black top with two white bands on the red, and the base of ST. RONAN's funnel appears yellow rather than red. Furness, Withy bought the ship in 1894, without changing her name, but when sold to D/S Urania, managed by A. Christensen of Copenhagen, in 1899 she became ORION. Her luck ran out at this point, and the iron steamer was wrecked on 1st June 1899 at Freshwater Point, Newfoundland whilst on passage from New York to Copenhagen with general cargo. Two-cylinder compound engines were supplied by her builders and, somewhat surprisingly for a relatively big ship, these were never tripled. *[Peter Newall collection]*

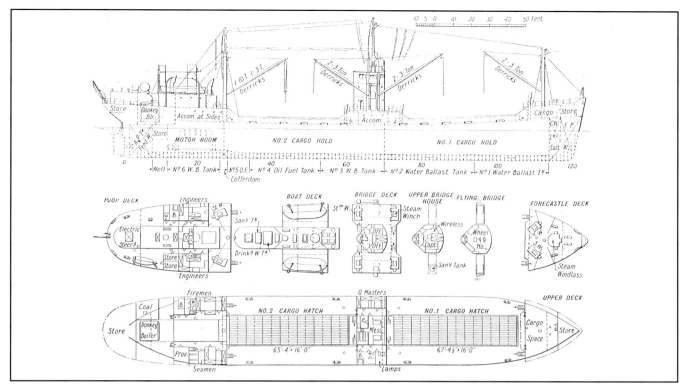

JACATRA (opposite page bottom)
William Hamilton and Co. Ltd., Port Glasgow; 1912, 5,373gt, 420 feet

Two twin-funnel vessels of N.V. Rotterdamsche Lloyd have been brought to our attention by readers, and whilst no photograph of the BROMO (3,217/1888) suitable for reproduction has come to light, we have been very fortunate to borrow this one of JACATRA. Purchased on the stocks by the Dutch owners, she had been laid down as SAINT THEODORE, suggesting that she too might have been destined for Rankin, Gilmour. The rareness of this photograph no doubt stems from the short peacetime career JACATRA: she was torpedoed by U 21 on 22nd February 1917, thirty miles west of Bishop Rock.

As Martin Lindenborn pointed out on page 189 of *Record 7*, after prolonged negotiations the Germans reluctantly replaced the group of no fewer than seven neutral Dutch ships illegally sunk by this submarine. One of these replacements was Hapag's WESTMARK (5,870/1914), unable to return to Germany and laid up at Sabang, and which received the name JACATRA when delivered to Holland. This has led to some confusion, and Duncan Haw's *Merchant Fleets in Profile 4* wrongly illustrates the WESTMARK as having the two funnel profile of the ship shown here. Arnold Kludas's *Der Schiffe der Hamburg-Amerika Linie 1907-1926* has a photograph of the newly-built WESTMARK which confirms that she had only one funnel. *[Martin Lindenborn collection]*

HYOGO MARU and OSAKA MARU (top)
Kasado Dock Co., Kasadoshima, Japan; 1935, 1,472gt, 252 feet

The exhaust for a donkey boiler gave a number of ships a two funnel appearance, including two interesting Japanese motorships built in the mid-1930s. *Shipping Wonders of the World,* from where the illustration comes, explains that the exhaust from their six-cylinder oil engines was taken into the larger, forward funnel, whilst that aft supplied the Scotch donkey boiler which served various steam winches. These ships were not alone in the 1930s as being curious hybrids: several early European motor ships benefited from the economy of a diesel engine for main propulsion, but still had to carry bunker coal and firemen. In other respects the two Japanese ships were well-designed: the long, clear hatches were suitable for timber or long, unwieldy cargoes like railway carriages. The description also mentions a lattice structure amidships to support the derricks, but we are left in ignorance of what this looked like, as no photographs of these ships have come to light, even though one of them had a long career. The OSAKA MARU foundered off Shiomisaki on 26th October 1936 whilst carrying Korean ore to Yokohama, but her sister HYOGO MARU remained in *Lloyd's Register* until 1966 when she is reported as being broken up. Survival of a Japanese merchant ship through the Second World War was exceptional, such was the destruction wrought by US submarines and aircraft and the indifference shown by the Japanese military to the protection of the vessels which were essential to maintaining their war. Perhaps the re-engining of HYOGO MARU in 1944 suggests a reason for her survival: an unreliable engine which restricted her voyaging?

XIN HUA No.5 (bottom)
Zhonghua Shipyard, Shanghai; 1977, 2,715gt, 101 metres

With his photograph taken at Hong Kong in November 1981, John B. Hill convinces us that the twin-funnel cargo ship still lives. XIN HUA No.5, owned by the People's Republic of China, is driven by a 6-cylinder Hudong Shipyard diesel, so the forward funnel is, presumably, an exhaust for a diesel auxiliary. The Zhonghua and Hudong yards, both in Shanghai, built at least ten ships to these dimensions, presumably to the same design. This ship was renamed YANG ZI JIANG 2 in 1982, when ownership was transferred to the China Yangtze River Shipping Co of Wuhan, for whom she continues in service. *[John B. Hill]*

PERTHSHIRE

R. and W. Hawthorn, Leslie and Co. Ltd., Hebburn; 1893, 5,574gt, 420 feet

Although not a two-funneller, PERTHSHIRE is included here because of the interest in her generated by a mention of her non-identical sister BUTESHIRE. In his letter below, Michael Charles offers some thoughts on the ship. She was built for the Elderslie Steamship Co. Ltd., a company managed by Turnbull, Martin and Co., and on this company's acquisition by Cayzer, Irvine and Co. in 1910, the rather appropriate title Scottish Shire Line Ltd. was adopted. The PERTHSHIRE was hired by the Admiralty in 1914 and initially used as a dummy battleship, being made to resemble HMS VANGUARD. Bought outright by the Admiralty in September 1915, she was converted to become the Coaling Officer's ship at Scapa Flow, carrying canteen stores, fresh water (some sources describe her as a water carrier at this stage of her career), and 1,500 tons of fuel oil. In March 1920 she became an oiler, and in 1922 a store carrier. The photograph of her at Malta shows her in her last guise: notes by Captain Sigwart on the back of the prints suggest that the black livery was applied when she was refitted in 1924/25 for a role as Mediterranean Fleet supply ship. PERTHSHIRE continued in His Majesty's service until replaced by the RFA RELIANT in February 1934, after which she was broken up at Spezia.

PERTHSHIRE painted by C. Kensington. *[British Mercantile Marine Memorial Collection]*

PERTHSHIRE and Gellatly, Hankey

PERTHSHIRE, sister ship to BUTESHIRE, is referred to as having 'been built with the stove pipe for the donkey boiler clamped to her funnel'. In the British Mercantile Marine Memorial Collection is a painting of her signed by the London-based ship portrait artist, C. Kensington, and dated 1895, which shows her in what appears to be that configuration (reproduced at the top of the page). Her owners are said to have found this ugly, but to my eye the portrait suggests that this slender flue, attached to the forepart of the funnel, is agreeably balanced aesthetically by a marginally broader steam-pipe positioned abaft of the funnel and slightly proud of it. Certainly I, for one, regard this as much more pleasing overall than the unmatching – and no doubt costly – additional funnel adopted for BUTESHIRE. Incidentally, your photographs of BUTESHIRE/BOLLINGTON GRANGE show her flush-decked and without provision for wind propulsion, whereas Kensington depicts PERTHSHIRE as having two short well-decks forward of the foremast and abaft the mainmast, thus conforming with Duncan Haws' profile (page 127 in *Merchant Fleets No. 33*). Kensington's portrait also shows her with four yards crossed on her foremast, fore-topmast and fore-topgallant staysails and a main-topmast staysail.

There *is* a company history of Gellatly, Hankey & Co. Ltd. It was written by George Blake and was published in 1962 by Blackie & Son Ltd. under the title *Gellatly's 1862-1962*. Its sixth chapter is devoted to and headed *The Mogul Steamship Company* and in this appears the book's only reference to the two-funnelled SIKH. '. . .she was unusual in a merchant fleet in having two funnels so markedly oval in form that one recorder describes them as looking 'like two Egyptian cigarettes.' Apparently she was built to carry Chinese coolie labour to South African gold and diamond mines, but that movement of population having been stopped as the result of popular outcry, Gellatly's flagship went to the Hamburg Amerika Company.'

Just one other quick comment on *Record* 8: whereas on page 198 you refer to the renamed CROFTON HALL as COMMERCIAL TRAVELLER, the photograph of the vessel in that later guise on page 199 clearly shows that the second word of her new name is in fact spelled in the American fashion, TRAVELER.

MICHAEL W.S. CHARLES, British Mercantile Marine Memorial Collection, 28 Queen's Square, Chippenham, Wiltshire SN15 3BL.

The photograph of COMMERCIAL TRAVELER should have been credited to Eric Johnson, courtesy William Schell: apologies to both gentlemen.

BOMBAY, FLORIDA and HONG MOH

Both these ships were chartered to Shaw Savill & Albion in 1883/4 to carry on its steam service to New Zealand before the new fleet was delivered. Note the Shaw Savill houseflag flying from the mainmast in each photo. The photographs would have been taken in the Thames prior to sailing and are probably by Gould of Gravesend.

Does the HONG MOH meet your definition of a cargo liner? She hardly had limited passenger accommodation as she carried thousands of Chinese coolies between Chinese and Straits ports.

BILL LAXON, Waimarana, Upper Whangateau Road, PO Box 171, Matakana 1240, New Zealand

CROFTON HALL

I agree that the amount of superstructure on CROFTON HALL gives the impression of passenger accommodation. I was interested to see that the HOWICK

HALL has portholes throughout the length of her upper 'tween deck. I know that some of the old British India cargo ships were also fitted in a like manner and were occasionally used for the pilgrim trade, and the passengers were unberthed in the tween deck, which normally carried cargo. In this case, additional lifeboats were also fitted as a temporary measure. Could Dunns be considering a similar trade, perhaps migrant workers to the United States? They would probably not have had to fit more lifeboats, as their ships were built before the introduction of the TITANIC rules for life-saving apparatus.
TONY SMYTHE, 35 Avondale Road, Rayleigh, Essex SS6 8NJ.

TABARISTAN
I was told that the two funnel arrangement was tried to see if improvements could be made to boiler room ventilation and to lessen corrosion.
ALAN McCLELLAND, 33 Montclair Drive, Mossley Hill, Liverpool L18 0HB.

LENNEP and GREIF
I feel I should draw your attention to some speculation concerning DADG's LENNEP (*Record* 8, page 197). That this name should be chosen as the name of the Dutch author since there might be an intention to sell her to the Netherlands is incorrect. Lennep at that time was the chief town of a district with 12,000 inhabitants, although today it is merely a suburb of the town of Remscheid. So LENNEP as a name was fully in line with DADG's naming habits.

At the top of page 197 is mentioned GRIEF ex GUBEN. In fact, the correct spelling is GREIF, meaning griffin or vulture.
PAUL KÖNIG, Berliner Strasse 19, D-52428 Jülich, Germany

SUD-EXPRESO and SUD-AMERICANO
John B. Hill sent further information about these ships from Ivarans Rederi 1920-1995 *by Bård Kolltveit, published 1995.*

The SUD-EXPRESO and SUD-AMERICANO were ordered as part of a major expansion of Ivaran's services, and were designed to accommodate 21 passengers. Delivery was originally scheduled for 1928, but there were severe delays, partly due to a shipyard strike, but mainly because of difficulties with the machinery. There were frequent breakdowns, even whilst the motors were still on the testbed in the engine shop. But as the vessels represented a major order, as well as technical prestige, Deutsche Werke made frantic efforts to remedy the problems. Nevertheless, Ivaran's technical consultants were sceptical, and Christensen, the owner, restated his right to refuse delivery of the second ship if the performance of SUD AMERICANO's machinery should fall short of that promised.

Formal trials in June 1929 and a demonstration to the press a week later went well, and an average maximum speed of 18.1 knots was achieved with vibrations from the big two-stroke diesels being almost unnoticeable. SUD AMERICANO lost no time in heading out to take up her express service between New York, Rio, Santos, Montevideo and Buenos Aires. Barely six weeks later, SUD EXPRESO performed equally well on her trials, and followed her sister.

However, it soon became evident that neither vessel could fulfil the contract speed of 16 knots without overworking the machinery. There were repeated breakdowns, with corresponding interruptions in the advertised sailing schedules. Both ships were withdrawn from the service in August 1930 and brought to Norway, where they were laid up side by side at Oslo whilst a lengthy and acrimonious arbitration process took place between owner and builder.

Ivar Christensen was accused of trying to refuse the vessels simply because he could not pay the installments on them: a cunning defence as the owner was under some financial pressure, having taken five new ships in under two years. The shipyard claimed that the vessels' masters had deliberately chosen circuitous routes to disrupt schedules. However, the court of arbitration in Hamburg did not accept these pleas, and ruled that Deutsche Werke had to take the ships back and pay compensation of 1.4 million Norwegian kroner for each vessel. In January 1931, the SUD-EXPRESO and SUD-AMERICANO left Oslo for Kiel.

Acknowledgements
In addition to those mentioned in the text, the editors would like to thank John Bartlett, James Cooper, Peter Newall, Bill Schell and Tony Smith for their help and suggestions. Ian Farquhar also came up with lists and photographs of Australian coastal vessels which had twin funnels, but we have decided to hold over this rather heterogenous group (which includes vesssels with substantial passenger accommodation) and use it as a basis of future article, which should help satisfy those who, following Peter Newall's feature on South African coasters in *Record* 8, expressed interest in similar pieces on Australian coastal vessels.

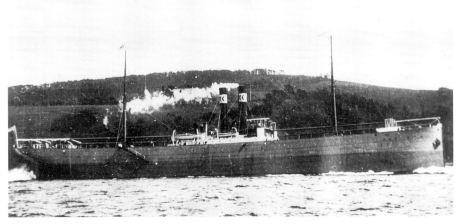

And finally, a mystery. Tony Smith found this photograph amongst material donated to the World Ship Photo Library by Captain John Isherwood, well-known for his inimitable and long-running 'Steamers of the Past' series in *Sea Breezes*. The ship is noted as ARABISTAN and appears to have Strick Line's funnel and hull colours, but this by no means sufficiently identifies her, as Strick used this name no fewer than nine times. All but two can be eliminated from photographs in Harold Appleyard's *Frank C. Strick & Co.* and other books. The candidates are the first ARABISTAN (3,194/1893), built by A. Stephen and Sons, Glasgow and sold to Italy as GIANO in 1910, only to be wrecked in December 1912; and the second ARABISTAN (2,891/1901) from William Pickersgill and Sons, Sunderland, sold to Greek owners as EUXEINOS in 1911 and sunk by the German submarine UB 53 in the Aegean in March 1918. However, Harold Appleyard expresses doubts about it being a Strick vessel, pointing out that the chevrons on the funnel appear the wrong way round, and that Strick's blue chevrons were fairly pale, whilst those in the photograph appear dark. In fact, close examination reveals that the funnel colours in the photograph have been retouched!

Incidentally, an ARABESTAN has already featured in this series, the former SIKH of Gellatly, Hankey; but this has a very different profile with distinctive wells fore and aft. Any offers for the identification of this ship?

THE PORT OF WIDNES
Part One
Albert Constable

Of the Mersey's small ports, Widnes has received the least attention from port historians. The port was ideally placed to serve the industry of south west Lancashire, and at times it prospered enormously, having three docks in its heyday. Despite inadequate facilities, and the difficulties of navigating the Upper Mersey, the port survived until the construction of the Runcorn-Widnes road bridge in the 1960s. This account by the last manager of a Widnes dock is believed to be the first time the port's full history has been told.

Building the docks at Widnes acted as a catalyst to the development of the town. As late as the 1830s, the land it now stands on - immediately north of the geological fault known as the Runcorn Gap, through which the Mersey flows - was purely agricultural. The nearest settlements, Appleton and Farnworth, were a mile or more to the north. On the south side of the river stood the growing town and port of Runcorn.

The Sankey Brook Navigation

The growth of Liverpool in the mid-eighteenth century meant a demand for coal for many local industries: salt refining, sugar baking, glass and pottery making, and brewing. Domestic demand for coal was also increasing, and there was trade to the north west coast and Ireland. The inability to transport sufficient quantities of coal from the mines around St. Helens to meet the demand led a group of Liverpool merchants and St. Helens' colliery owners, supported by Liverpool Corporation, to build a canal between St. Helens and the River Mersey, near Warrington. Completed in 1757, the canal linked with a one-and-a-half-mile navigable section of Sankey Brook at the Mersey end.

In 1772 the Sankey Brook Navigation was extended by about two miles to a new lock on the Mersey at Fiddlers Ferry, as there was insufficient water in the river above this point, especially at neap tides. Although it was suggested at this time that the canal be extended to Runcorn Gap to enable craft to avoid the most difficult stretches of the Upper Mersey, the Canal Company did not act on this advice. Despite the extension to Fiddlers Ferry, there were still problems as a quotation from the early part of the nineteenth century indicates: '... trips betwixt Runcorn and Fiddler's Ferry are made with great difficulty owing to the shallow water and narrow channels, combined with the number of vessels

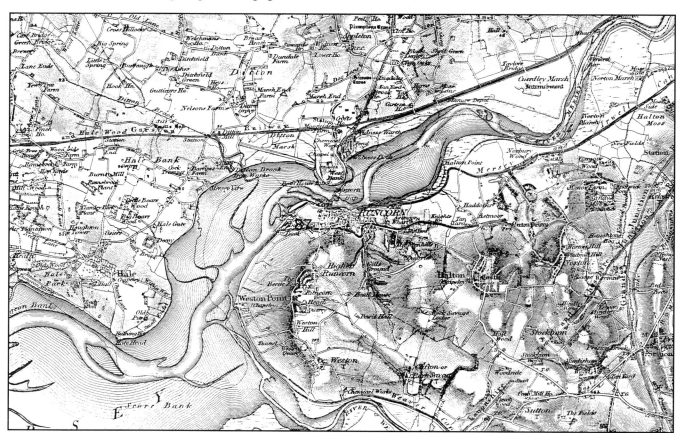

The Upper Mersey from an Ordnance Survey map published in 1842, with the Sankey Navigation running from top right and, alongside it, the railway from St. Helens which had recently been extended beyond Widnes to Garston. 'Widness' is shown well to the north, although Widness Dock is marked at the point where the original St. Helens and Runcorn Gap Railway reached tidewater. To the south, Runcorn is already a sizeable town. *[Author's collection]*

grounded each tide'. In 1819 the Canal Company did try to obtain an Act for an extension to Runcorn Gap, but were unsuccessful.

Two Acts, two docks

In 1830 two Acts of Parliament were passed on the same day, 29th May. One authorised a railway from St. Helens to Runcorn Gap, where there was to be a dock capable of taking up to 40 vessels of a maximum size of 300 tons. The other Act, stimulated by the railway proposal, was for an extension of Sankey Brook Navigation some three and a half miles to the Mersey at Runcorn Gap, where there was to be another dock. There were to be twin locks into the Mersey, 79 x 20 feet, and the dock was to be created by widening the canal to about 110 feet for its final 800 feet. Both the railway and the canal extension were completed in mid-1833, giving two docks at Runcorn Gap.

There was a considerable contrast in the facilities of the two docks. The canal company provided little if any cargo handling equipment, work being done by the ship's crew using the ship's gear. The dock belonging to the St. Helens and Runcorn Gap Railway Company – the first to be owned and operated by a railway, and known both as the Railway Dock and as Widnes Dock – had dimensions of approximately 265 x 215 feet, with a lock about 97 x 24 feet. It had a series of reception sidings each with its own coal chute to handle the dock's principle commodity, coal being its *raison d'etre*. Small steam and hand cranes were also provided to handle materials for the growing glass, copper and alkali industries of St. Helens.

Despite these new facilities, there were still problems. Firstly, vessels could not always move between the Mersey and the Railway Dock or the Canal. At neap tides, there was only four feet of

Above: Mersey flats and other craft in the St. Helens Canal (formerly the Sankey Navigation), in the 1890s. To provide dock facilities, the canal at Widnes was simply built wider at this point. Right: flats in the Mersey waiting to enter the Canal or Railway Dock. [Both: Author's collection]

water over the cills, and movements could be made only two hours each side of high water. No movements at all were possible on about 80 days each year. The second problem was over-capacity. The result was a price war, which meant both the railway and canal companies neglected the maintenance of their facilities. The outcome was an amalgamation in 1845 to form a new company, the St. Helens Canal and Railway Company.

The new company's first project was to extend its railway to Garston, some eight miles downstream, and build a dock capable of handling much larger vessels than could reach Widnes. The Act of Parliament for these new works stipulated that the existing facilities of canal and dock at Widnes must be maintained. In the rates schedule attached to the Act charges were specified for statutory tons of 20 cwts. During price wars between the canal and railway, the position had been reached where a one ton rate was being charged for 30 cwts of goods. The amalgamated company brought the new charges into operation on all its existing facilities, which represented a 50% increase in rates.

The amalgamation meant that land held at Widnes was more than required for operations, and some could be released for industrial development.

Widnes grows, the old docks decline

In 1847 the 22-year old John Hutchinson left his job as Manager of Kurtz's alkali works at St. Helens and opened a factory to produce alkali by the Leblanc process on land between the Canal and the Railway Dock in Widnes. This site had enormous economic advantages over St. Helens. Not only was the land cheap, but major savings on transport costs of raw materials could also be achieved. To produce one ton of alkali required 12-14 tons of raw materials, including 5-6 tons of coal, plus salt, limestone and pyrites, and all this had to be moved from Widnes to St. Helens. The economic advantages of Widnes over St. Helens were soon recognised by others, and the town grew quickly as alkali and other factories were set up adjacent to the canal or railway. Such was its expansion that, by the 1870s, Widnes had become the major centre of alkali manufacture in the United Kingdom, with large quantities going for export. The docks and railways served these industries with many manufacturers having preferential berths for loading and discharging their own cargoes.

Towards the end of the eighteenth century, manufacture of alkali by the environmentally-damaging Leblanc process went into serious decline as other methods became available, and Widnes docks' trade withered away. After the First World War the Railway Dock was principally used to discharge sand dredged from the Mersey, and in 1933 it was closed and filled in. Upper sections of the canal began to be closed soon after the First World War, until by the 1950s only that between Widnes and Sankey was operational. All movements on the canal ceased in 1959 when the last user, a sugar refiner at Sankey, transferred his traffic to the road. The canal was abandoned in 1963. However, the final 400 yards of the canal has since been cleaned and one lock made operational for use as a marina. The shallow water in the dock is now a leisure facility. Together, these make up the area known as Spike Island: the word spike being used by workmen in the early days of the dock to refer to lodgings.

An aerial view of Widnes believed to date from about 1919. This is the only photograph known which shows craft in the Railway or Widnes Dock, right of centre. The large expanse of water beyond and to the left of this dock is its reservoir. The St. Helens Canal can also be clearly seen, curving round top left. *[Author's collection]*

Another view of the St. Helens Canal at Widnes with few craft but with the alkali factory chimneys in full production. Widnes had a well-deserved reputation for pollution, and in the 1870s this was instrumental in producing the first Act of Parliament designed to protect the environment, and which established the Alkali Inspectorate. *[Author's collection]*

West Bank Dock

The rapid growth of Widnes in the mid nineteenth century led to a shortage of suitable land for development by firms anxious to begin manufacture in the area. In 1862 John Hutchinson acquired some 350 acres of land downstream of Runcorn Gap and created what was probably the United Kingdom's first industrial estate with its own private railway and dock. It was this dock, West Bank Dock, which outlived its rivals, and is the only one for which extensive documentation has survived. There were a number of constraints on the development of the dock and the adjoining industrial estate. The land was generally some six feet lower than the Widnes to Garston railway line, much of it actually being foreshore, and all being covered by water during higher tides. The dock was formed partly by excavation and partly by building up the adjoining land, and the finished site needed protection from the river, which was built up over a long period. In addition to the poor quality of the land, further constraints were the financial situation of the owners whose business was expanding in other ways at the time, and the construction of the viaduct required by the Widnes to Runcorn rail bridge, opened in 1868.

West Bank Dock became operational in August 1864. It was then little more than a walled stream with a dam at one end and a gate at the other. Its dimensions were 200 x 110 feet, and the walls on the east side were load-bearing, whilst those on the west side required crane stages. The dock gate was 35 feet wide and its cill six feet above the cill of Liverpool Old Dock.

Figures for the first few months of operation give an indication of the dock's traffic. In September 1864, Samuel Stock shipped out 1,046 tons of coal; Hutchinson imported 737 tons of salt and ore for his own factories; and alkali manufacturers Gaskell, Deacon & Co. imported 119 tons of what was described as 'kelp salt' in the Kirkwall-registered schooner MARGARET TRAILL (79/1862). This would be potassium chloride, as opposed to sodium chloride, derived from seaweed and used in the manufacture of more expensive soaps. The total traffic for September was 1,902 tons, and this grew to 2,122 tons in October. In this month, 589 tons of iron ore was imported for the West Bank Iron Company in four vessels whose names were so common that it is difficult to guess which individual craft were involved: ANN, FANNY, WILLIAM and MARY. In November 1864 a charge was made for 25 tons of coal shipped to the GEORGE, suggesting that it was steam vessel requiring bunkers. The most likely candidate of this name, the first recorded steamer at Widnes, was a Liverpool-registered vessel of 90 tons built in 1834. In 1865, the first full year of operation, over 40,000 tons were handled. It was rare for vessels using the dock to bring in a cargo and take one out, and of the 23 vessels using the dock in July 1865 only the ANN & ELLEN did so, bringing in ore and loading coal.

In 1865 John Hutchinson died at the age of 40 and his business interests were taken over by his trustees, a change which was to affect the operation and development of West Bank Dock for many years. The trustees installed one of their number, Major James Cross, as manager. He had been the Chief Engineer to the St. Helens and Runcorn Gap Railway until its absorption into the London & North Western Railway in 1864, so was well aware of the dock facilities at Widnes and Garston, and the problems of the Upper Mersey.

Traffic increased each year except 1866, and by 1868 throughput had reached 100,000 tons. Traffic figures indicated that, despite the intention that the dock would serve the industrial estate, it was also handling traffic that previously used Widnes Dock and the canal. Coal was shipped out in increasing quantities. Works with their own unloading facilities on the canal were moving material through West Bank Dock despite the rail

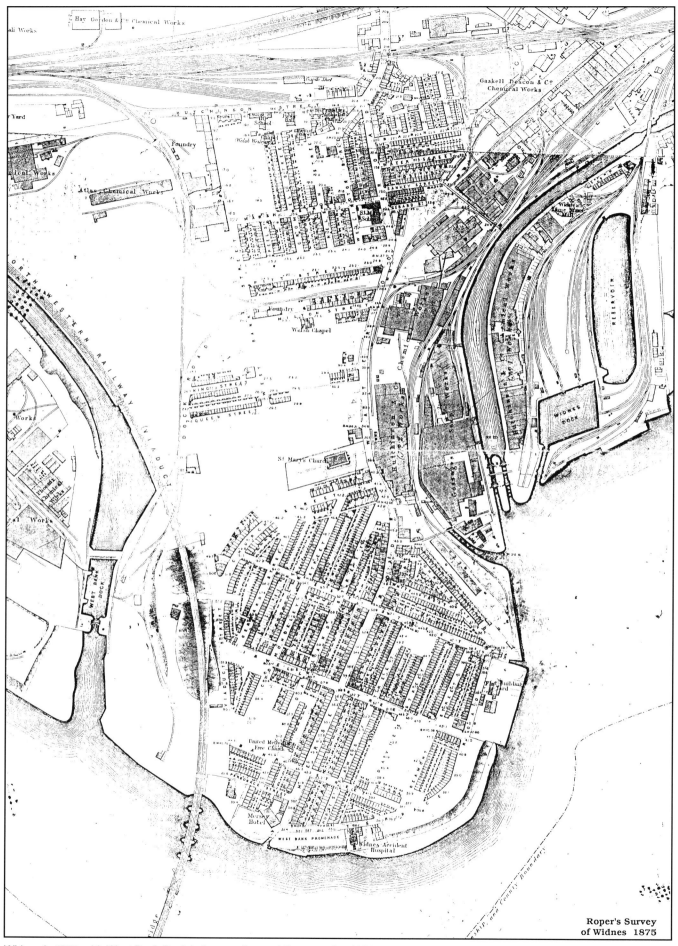

Roper's Survey
of Widnes 1875

Widnes in 1875, with West Bank Dock in its original, unimproved state. The extensive railway sidings serving Widnes Dock are apparent. Hutchinson's Chemical Works occupy the site between this dock and sidings and the canal. *[Author's collection]*

movements that this required, including white sand and river sand for the glass industry in St. Helens, for local soap manufacturers and the construction industry. White sand from Scotland was shipped in Mersey flats including BRITANNIA, HUGH, MARIA, TOM, and WELLINGTON.

A hand-operated tip for end-door coal wagons was installed and began operation in September 1867, positioned to suit the hatches on steam barges. Surviving correspondence relates that 200 tons of coal was loaded into one steam barge, between 9.00 am and 2.00 pm, despite an hour being lost because of the need to shunt coal wagons which were the wrong way round. Both the captain of the vessel and the agent were pleased with the loading rate and the lack of breakage of the coal. The steamer was probably the BLACK DIAMOND, owned by Richard Evans of Winsford, loading coal from Samuel Stock's colliery.

Problems and proposals

In 1868 there were renewed reports of problems with the sand banks in the Upper Mersey off both the Canal and the Railway Dock, with a vessel loaded with chemicals being aground for over a week. There was also under-capacity: West Bank Dock introduced night working, but still could not cope with the demand. To add to the local problems, the LNWR suffered a sudden shortage of coal wagons, which resulted in their charges for coal shipped through Garston being set lower than for that through Widnes. The price of coal in the Widnes area rocketed, and had a knock-on effect on the chemical industry, reducing output and demand for raw materials.

Three proposals were made in the 1870s to deal with the problems. First, Major Cross proposed that West Bank Dock be enlarged at its southern end, and given a new gate to the river. His fellow trustees were sympathetic to the idea, but their preferred solution was to sell the dock if a buyer could be found. The finances of the Hutchinson Trust were such that money was not available for Cross's proposed enlargement.

Undeterred, Cross in his capacity as a leading figure in both business and civic communities suggested building a branch line from the Cheshire Lines Committee railway between Liverpool and Manchester which ran to the north of Widnes. The proposed branch would link West Bank Dock and a new dock to be built downstream at Ditton Brook. The proposal for the dock came to nothing, but the railway was built in the late 1870s and proved important for the development of West Bank Dock, giving it a connection for traffic from Yorkshire and Derbyshire.

The third proposal was to extend the Sankey Canal some three miles downstream to Hale Head, where the Upper Mersey channel was much better than at Widnes. The extension would have passed through West Bank Dock, and used certain arches of the railway viaduct which had been built to such a specification that they could be used by canal traffic. This proposal was put in front of Parliament in both the 1872-73 and 1873-74 sessions, but failed due to opposition from the Mersey Conservator and the Mersey Docks and Harbour Board.

Few figures are available for trade in the early 1870s, but the table below shows the movements for the 12 months ending September 1879. These suggest that about one third of the vessels loaded one way only. The average tonnage was less than 100. Figures for the six month period from October 1879 to March 1880 show that traffic was dominated by coal, which made up 76% of the outward traffic of almost 20,000 tons. The only other significant outward cargo was chemicals, mainly superphosphates. Inward cargoes, totalling over 16,000 tons during this period, were river (or red) sand and white sand, making up about 35% of the total, plus phosphates, salt and salt cake, iron and copper ore, bricks, limestone, pig iron, pit props, nitre, and stones.

Movements and tonnages for the 12 months ending 30th September 1879

	Inward	Outward	Total
Light vessels	445	321	766
Loaded vessels	414	593	1,067
Tonnage	40,540	52,125	92,665

West Bank Dock extended

John Hutchinson's will was contested in the Chancery Court in 1878, and this restricted the decisions which Major Cross could take. The Court would not sanction repairs to the dock gates, and in 1879 Cross complained that the dock was little more than a tidal creek. It is not known how long this situation persisted, but in 1880 110,000 tons was shipped through the dock. In that year the dock's financial constraints were eased, with the sale of Hutchinson's alkali works which had been losing money. The improved financial position and upturn in trade persuaded Cross to make fresh proposals to extend the dock. These were more ambitious than previous proposals, envisaging an extension on the scale planned by John Hutchinson. Cross made bullish but detailed estimates of throughput after the extension, looking forward to annual inward cargoes totalling 270,000 tons, and outward of 223,000. The total of 493,000 was over four times the throughput for 1880.

Despite their inability to sanction minor repairs, the Chancery Court gave permission for the extension to proceed, and in January 1883 the dock was closed for the work to be carried out. The dam at the north end of the existing dock was removed and the dock extended northward, and alongside the railway viaduct to a total of some 600 yards. The dock was also extended to the south and an arm dug to the west, giving a total water area of 41,000 square yards compared to the original 2,800. The original gates were overhauled, and the cill lowered by 18 inches. The coal tip was replaced and repositioned but no other mechanical equipment was purchased.

The dock reopened in May 1884, and the tonnage handled rapidly increased, reaching over 400,000 tons in 1889, four times that before the alterations, and almost up to Cross's estimate. In 1888 2,950 sailing vessels carried 300,000 tons and 516 steamers 64,000 tons. Vessels carrying 200 tons were regularly using the dock, and larger ones could be dealt with. A new problem faced the Dock Master: shortage of berths, with vessels waiting two to three days to enter the dock. An 1889 report advised that

14 vessels were waiting to enter the dock and 11 were already in dock awaiting a berth. In addition, a further problem arose: not all vessels wishing to enter or leave on certain tides can do so because of the time that the gates would have had to be opened.

As elsewhere, the practice was introduced of giving steamers preference over sailing vessels, but this was later modified so that a vessel would not be required to give way to the same vessel more than once during any visit to the dock. Not surprisingly, this caused many problems for the dock gatemen and others. Around 1889 appear the first reports of coal being loaded onto barges to be lightered to larger ships lying in the river off Liverpool.

[To be continued]

A superb view of steam and sailing craft crowding West Bank Dock. The coastal sailing craft in the background cannot be identified, but the steamer to the right is believed to be the CECIL (235/1890) owned by Brundrit and Co., Runcorn. Names can be discerned on two of the three flats in the foreground: PILOT and THOMAS. *[Author's collection]*

PUTTING THE RECORD STRAIGHT

Letters, additions, amendments and photographs relating to articles in any issues of *Record* are welcomed. Letters may be lightly edited.

Engine too powerful

As a follow-up to your Anchor-Brocklebank history *(Ships in Focus Anchor and Brocklebank Lines)* the following information – new to me, certainly – was noted in *Engineer,* 16th July 1920 and may be of interest. After 10,000 miles, FULLAGAR had given satisfactory service, and Brocklebank decided that her experimental opposed-piston engine was needlessly powerful for a ship of her type. They then placed an order for a similar engine which, along with that originally fitted in the FULLAGAR, would be installed in a 4,000-ton ship which was currently under construction. Cammell Laird confirmed that they had in hand twin-screw machinery of the same type of about 2,000 bhp to go into a ship being built for Brocklebank, and that the FULLAGAR engine in the ship of that name was to be replaced by another lower-powered engine. The FULLAGAR had been built under the supervision of G.S. Goodwin, Brocklebank's technical advisors, and was then bought by them, it would appear from that statement that she was not originally ordered by the company but possibly built *on spec* by the shipbuilders

to prove the engine.
JAMES A. POTTINGER, 1 Jesmond Circle, Bridge of Don, Aberdeen AB22 8WX.
The two Fullagar engines presumably went into Brocklebank's MALIA (3,872/1921), built at Port Glasgow. However, these engines gave only two years' service before they were replaced. Cammell Lairds may have launched FULLAGAR on spec, but as soon as she was completed in July 1920 she was registered in the ownership of Thos. and Jno. Brocklebank Ltd. Editor.

Too late for lighthouses

For me *Record* 8 was a really good edition: I loved the photos of Hull, full of fascinating details like the way cargo used to be handled, and of the atmosphere of 'the good old days'. In response your postscript on page 217, I for one would welcome more on British-built Greek ships.

The photo of LA MARGUERITE *(Record* 8) shows her late in her career, when the lighthouses, which were prominent features mounted on the fore sides of the paddleboxes, had been removed and replaced by conventional sidelights mounted on the bridge wings. The latter had also acquired cabs.
TONY SMYTHE, 35 Avondale Road, Rayleigh, Essex SS6 8NJ.

British money, Greek tramp?

One aspect of the apparent desire of Greek shipowners to order their ships from British yards was the availability of funds accumulated during the war. Kulukundis in his *Ships loved and painted* writes: 'Greeks who had lost their ships had large sterling holdings which were not convertible and non-exportable. Replacement of their ships outside the UK was impossible'. To what extent did this influence the apparent enthusiasm with which the Greek shipowners ordered their ships in this country after the war, I wonder?

Captain Kinghorn's Coaly Tyne article brought back many memories, but as an engineer I must point out a couple of omissions in his record of Tyneside engine builders. At St. Peters, near Newcastle, was the works of Hawthorn, Leslie. Apart from engining most of the ships built at Hebburn, they produced many diesel engines, including those under licence from Werkspoor (mainly for Shell tankers), Sulzer and Doxford. They also constructed many high-power sets of turbine machinery for warships.

The other company to which I refer is John Readhead, whose engine works adjoined his shipyard at South Shields. Whilst Readheads did not supply engines to other builders, they did produce triple-expansion machinery and boilers for practically every ship built at West Docks until the shipyard started to construct diesel-engined ships, when the supply of machinery was contracted to others.

JOHN B. HILL, The Hollies, Wall, Hexham, Northumberland NE46 4EQ.

The Dukes of Trent

I was particularly interested in 'British yard, Greek tramp' in *Record* 8, as I served in two of Livanos' ships of the London-based Trent Maritime Co. Ltd. which was run, if I remember correctly, by Nicholas Livanos. It was, in my opinion, a well-run and efficient little company, and I enjoyed my few years with them. I served as second mate on the DUKE OF ATHENS from 8th April 1946 to 28th August 1948, and as first mate on the DUKE OF SPARTA from 19th July 1949 to 16th January 1950. Like LUCY, neither of these ships had the white band which was general amongst the Livanos ships. I can't tell you why this practice was not carried out in this case, but it was possibly to distinguish the British-run ships under Trent Maritime from the rest of the Livanos fleet.

Capt. J.C. MORRIS, 5 Glen View Crescent, Heysham, Morecambe LA3 2QW.

Many readers expressed their interest in the article on British-built ships for the Greek flag, and Greek shipowning is a subject to which we intend to return.

Definitely a near miss

The photographer, John McRoberts, gave an account of the close-quarters situation seen in the photo in *Record* 7 in a letter to *Sea Breezes* in 1966. The MAURETANIA had been berthed port side to Princes Stage and, on sailing, backed off the Stage to manoeuvre clear of the ULLAPOOL wreck prior to swinging downstream. Unfortunately, at the same time MEMNON cleared Alfred Lock prior to proceeding seaward. The MEMNON got her way off with a good astern movement, and the MAURETANIA let go her stern tug and managed to get her head round downstream. This occurred in the days before VHF, but one can imagine the ripe language on both bridges!

Capt. V.W. PITCHER, FNI, Mandarin Lodge, The Street, Lower Halstow, Sittingbourne, Kent ME9 7DY.

MANZ observation

With reference to the letter from J.L.Loughran in *Record* 8 where he indicates that the flag flying at the main on the WENDOVER on page 125 of *Record* 6 is not the Port Line flag, it is in fact the MANZ Line flag. WENDOVER was chartered to Port Line in October 1956 for a round voyage on the Montreal Australia New Zealand Line Ltd. berth from Montreal to main New Zealand ports and return. This flag was the old T.B. Royden flag of blue top and red bottom with a white diamond in the centre: the white portion can be seen in the illustration.

IAN FARQUHAR, R.D.2, Dunedin, New Zealand

Manx omission

I was surprised that no mention was made in the Barrow article in *Records* 6 and 7 to the effect that the port was used extensively by the Isle of Man Steam Packet Company for laying up its steamers over the winter months. Towards the end of the 1930s the Steam Packet fleet numbered 15, and as many as ten of the steamers were laid up for almost nine months in every year: the majority at Barrow; the remainder at Birkenhead. Even in the post-war years, up to the end of the 1960s, at least four of the Manx fleet would spend their winter slumbers at Barrow. On the left-hand side of the photograph on the front cover of *Record* 7 the foremast and bridge of the 1905 VIKING, and the stern of the 1920 SNAEFELL (ex VIPER of 1906) can be seen.

JOHN SHEPHERD, Flat 7, Mount Court, Mount Road, Wallasey, Merseyside LA45 9JS.

SNAEFELL, built as VIPER for G. & J. Burns' Ardrossan to Belfast service, was bought by the IoMSPCo in 1920, and served them until 1945.

Another tanker that never was

John Hill's search for 'The tanker that never was' (*Record* 8) caught my eye as I had also noted the brief appearance of SCOTTISH HIGHLANDS in the fleet of Tankers Ltd. May I name the fourth tanker, courtesy of the 1923 *Lloyd's Confidential Index,* SCOTTISH MONARCH, a name which Raeburn and Verel were currently using. The inclusion of nearly-ready ships in the *Register* with minimal details was not new. In most cases the first supplement carried full details, but in a few cases sale and change of name resulted in fleeting entries.

The registered dimensions of LUBRAFOL are the same as SCOTTISH STRATH and CASTLE, and ATLANTIC was close so a warm day and human error with the tape can be blamed for any disparity. As regards machinery, much greater alterations were undertaken at times than would be required to change the steam triples for two Sulzer diesels, two model 4S60 for LUBRAFOL and a 6ST60 model for ATLANTIC.

The builder's berth records go a step towards confirming that these were the cancelled tankers. All four were built under joint classification of Lloyd's Register and the British Corporation, although their class was then allowed to expire. I have seen the British Corporation's hull and machinery reports for SCOTTISH STRATH, and the machinery report for LUBRAFOL. The STRATH's keel was laid on 20th October 1920, she was launched 29th December 1921, and ran trials on 11th July 1922. The first visit of the surveyor to inspect the LUBRAFOL's engines was on 6th August 1923, and the last on 6th December 1924. DAVID BURRELL, 63 Avisyard Avenue, Cumnock, Ayrshire KA18 3BJ.

Breaking at Barrow

I offer the following identifications for vessels seen in the aerial photograph of Barrow-in-Furness on page 176 of *Record* 7 (see photograph opposite):
(1) Captain class frigate HMS AFFLECK (1943) with her stern blown off. She was laid up at Barrow for most of 1945 and all of 1946.
(2) Destroyer HMS KEPPEL (1920) which arrived at Barrow in July 1945. Note oval funnels and two triple torpedo tube mounts.
(3) Destroyer HMS MALCOLM (1919) which arrived at Barrow on 25th July 1945. Note round funnels and only one triple torpedo tube mount. She is also very slightly longer than HMS KEPPEL.
(4) Destroyer HMS WHITEHALL (1919) also arrived at Barrow 25th July 1945. Note only one funnel and no torpedo tubes. She is the shortest of the four destroyers.
(5) Destroyer HMS DUNCAN (1932), which arrived at Barrow on 9th June 1945 and was paid off ten days later to Category C Reserve. She was sold to BISCO on 8th July 1945 and allocated to T.W Ward Ltd., but was still substantially intact as late as August 1948. Note that she is the same length as KEPPEL but is slightly beamier and has a quadruple bank of torpedo tubes.
(6) A naval minesweeping trawler, probably one of the Dance class but I cannot be certain as a large number of the war-built trawlers were very similar in layout.
(7) I believe this to be the EMPIRE JESSICA (2,890/1943).
(8) I believe this to be the SRECA (5,248/1918), a Yugoslav ship.
(9) I cannot come up with an identification for this vessel.
(10) I believe this is the THISTLEFORD (4,781/1928).
(11) An unidentified bucket dredger.

Other vessels in the photograph are three tugs and six coasters.
From *Lloyd's Shipping Index* and *Lloyd's List* the only deep sea vessels I have traced being at Barrow on 13th August 1945 are:
GOVERNOR (5,571/1918), arrived 28th April
EMPRESS OF RUSSIA (16,810/1913), arrived 9th June
THISTLEFORD (4,781/1928), arrived 29th July
SKARABORG (1,220/1914), arrived 6th August

Proving that views of her are not as rare as was suggested in *Record* 8, Terry Belt supplied this fine postcard showing SCOTTISH CASTLE as PETTER II in No. 1 Dry Dock at Falmouth. PETTER II lasted until broken up in 1954, and Terry dates the photograph to the late 1940s by the presence of the wreck of STANWOOD (4,158/1917), just to the right of the sailing vessel in the right background. This Billmeir steamer sank on 10th December 1939 after her cargo of coal caught fire. Falmouth's No. 1 Dry Dock is now partially covered, and operated by Pendennis Shipyard Ltd. *[Keith Hancock collection]*

EMPIRE JESSICA (2,890/1943), arrived 9th August
SRECA (5,248/1918), arrived 12th August.

The EMPRESS OF RUSSIA is obviously not in the picture and I cannot match the SKARABORG or the GOVERNOR to ship (9) on the photograph. I make no apologies for not even attempting to identify the coasters, tugs, and the dredger in the picture.
BOB G. TODD, Head of Historic Photographs & Ship Plans Section, National Maritime Museum, Greenwich, London SE10 9NF.

Bob's findings were shown to Ken Royall, who supplied many of the photographs for the Barrow article. The identification of the destroyers was masterly: Mr. Todd must have an excellent magnifying glass! However, I don't think that vessel (1) can be HMS AFFLECK, as the aerial view definitely shows a ship minus its stern and AFFLECK's stern was only buckled. It could be a sister ship, HMS REDMILL, whose stern was blown off by U 1105 on 27th April 1945. She was towed to Londonderry and later laid up at Barrow, but I have no arrival date. Or it could be HMS MANNERS, another Captain class frigate, whose stern was blown off by U 1172 on 26th January 1945. She was towed to Barrow to lay up, but again I have no arrival or departure dates.
KEN ROYALL, 184 Park Avenue, Barrow-in-Furness, Cumbria LA13 9BL.

From Guinness to water

Record 7 mentioned the Guinness barges. Because these are unregistered it is often difficult to trace their histories. However, from minute books and other records of the Tees Conservancy Commissioners (TCC) I can provide information about the KNOCKMAROON which spent the second half of her long life on the River Tees.

KNOCKMAROON was built by Vickers Ireland Ltd. at Dublin in 1929 for Guinness, Son & Co. Ltd. Her dimensions were 80.0 x 17.1 x 6.0 feet, gross tonnage 81, net 48, speed about 7 knots from a coal-burning steam

engine of 160 I.H.P.

By November 1949 she had moved out of Guinness ownership and belonged to John Hunt & Sons (Leeds) Ltd. In that month it was reported to the TCC Works Committee that KNOCKMAROON was on sale for £2,600 as and where lying in Leeds and was suitable for conversion as a water carrier. After negotiation she was secured for £2,350; the cost of towing her to the Tees, carrying out minor repairs and conversion for use as a water carrier being estimated at a further £950.

At the Works Committee meeting on 21st July 1950 it was reported that the conversion of the KNOCKMAROON for craft watering purposes had been completed at a total cost including purchase of £3,600 7s. 2d. She had a tank capacity of 60 tons of fresh water which could be discharged at a rate of about 40 tons per hour, and was to be used for supplying water to the Commissioners' dredging fleet, carriage of stores and light towage. She was put into service on the 20th June and from that date until the 14th July made 48 visits to the Commissioners' craft, during which she supplied 700 tons of fresh water.

On 1st January 1967 the KNOCKMAROON was transferred from the Tees Conservancy Commissioners to the newly-formed Tees and Hartlepools Port Authority (the 's' of Hartlepools disappeared a year or two later on the unification of the separate towns of West Hartlepool and Hartlepool as, simply, Hartlepool). She remained in commission until January 1968 and in June 1969 was sold to Tees Marine Services Ltd., Middlesbrough for £600 to be broken up.

Despite the KNOCKMAROON being on the Tees for 20 years, no photographs of her have been found. Several local historians would be extremely interested in obtaining such a photograph.
RON MAPPLEBECK, 8 St. Margarets Grove, Acklam, Middlesbrough TS5 7SB.

THE UPS AND DOWNS OF BARON VERNON
Colin Campbell and Roy Fenton

The article on Palmers of Boston and Ringaskiddy in *Record* 6 referred to salvage operations on the steamer BARON VERNON (2,603/1922) in the Clyde in 1923. Colin Campbell discovered the photographs of the salvage of this ship in the Glasgow Museum of Transport and in the Wotherspoon Collection in the Mitchell Library. Thanks to the Ballast Trust, they are reproduced here as a record of a remarkably long-drawn out epic of salvage

The steamer was launched on 18th October 1921 by Irvine's Shipbuilding & Dry Docks Co. Ltd., West Hartlepool as the DUNMORE HEAD for the Ulster Steamship Co. Ltd. Whilst still on the builders' hands, in February 1922 she was bought for the bargain price of £40,000 by Hugh Hogarth and Sons, who had her completed as BARON VERNON, registered as usual for this fleet in Ardrossan.

At 9.30 pm on 25th May 1923 the BARON VERNON was off Dumbarton during the last stage of a voyage from Bilbao to Glasgow with ore and esparto grass when she collided with the Canadian Pacific METAGAMA (12,420/1914), outward bound for Quebec with 1,100 passengers. Holed below the waterline and with her port bow stove in, the ore-laden BARON VERNON sank at Puddle Deep near Langbank. She posed a danger to navigation, and the very next day the British Marine Salvage Company began to discharge her cargo into lighters. However, by 29th March divers were reporting that the hull had sunk three feet further into the

mud despite the lightening operation. With further settling, and the hull showing signs of strain, the salvage company abandoned operations on 6th June.

The Clyde Navigation Trust sat on their hands for a while, and not until 28th June did they invite tenders for raising or removing the wreck from the fairway. In contracts dated 19th and 24th July, salvage contractors Thomas Ensor & Son of Queenstown undertook the job for £28,000 on a 'no cure, no pay' basis. Ensors were to bitterly regret winning this contract, as salvage proved to be the 'most arduous and difficult operation'.

After nine months work, Ensors reported on 30th April 1924 that the BARON VERNON's back was broken. Nevertheless, on 8th May they were able to lift the wreck sufficiently to move it about 20 feet towards shore and out of the navigation channel. A further attempt to lift her on 25th May was hampered by the remains of the esparto grass cargo clogging the pumps. On 24th June the wreck was raised sufficiently to allow strengthening work to be carried out on the deck. Not until 15th July - almost 14 months after she sank - was BARON VERNON completely raised and taken to No. 3 Graving Dock at Govan. The cost of the salvage operation had well exceeded the £28,000 paid by the Clyde Navigation Trust and helped put Thomas Ensor & Sons out of business.

On 23rd July the wreck was sold by auction, a David Dawson succeeding in buying her for £5,500. Her remaining cargo of about 1,400 tons of ore fetched a

further £260. The BARON DUNMORE was immediately moved out of the graving dock, presumably whilst the new buyer considered his options.

The photograph on page 56 shows just what damage a 12,420 ton liner can inflict on the bow of a small tramp. It can be dated to 2nd August 1924 by the presence of the Norwegian steamer LOVSTAKKEN (2,462/1921)

on Berth 24 further up Princes Dock: Clyde Trust record books reveal not just when a ship arrived, but what berth she used. The same records indicate that BARON VERNON moved to Berth 25 of Princes Dock that day. In the foreground at Berth 26 is the puffer RACHEL (87/1892) which had recently arrived from Carnlough with limestone. The name of the puffer further up the dock

cannot be read, but the Clyde Navigation records reveal that it is the HAFTON (81/1910), which arrived at Berth 25 that day with timber from Loch Sween.

On 14th August BARON VERNON returned to the Govan dry dock, presumably to be made fit for towing to Rotterdam, where Dawson had arranged to have her repaired. She was in dock for a further four days, and on 21st August left in tow of the Dutch tug HUMBER (519/1907). In Holland the hull was refurbished and lengthened to 326 feet, its gross tonnage becoming 2,743, and she emerged as DOWANHILL, registered in the ownership of the Dawson Shipping Co. Ltd. (Dawson

Brothers & Rowan, managers), Glasgow. In 1927 she was sold to French owners as MONCEAU, but returned to Britain in 1929 when bought by Constants (South Wales) Ltd. and renamed HAWKINGE. She was not to survive long: on 12th December 1929, whilst on passage from Lisbon to Bilbao in ballast, HAWKINGE was wrecked near Cape Finisterre.

A lot had been packed into a comparatively short career: five owners, five names, two serious accidents, a major expense to the Clyde Navigation Trust, and the bankrupting of her salvor.

SOURCES AND ACKNOWLEDGEMENTS

Photographs are from the collection of John Clarkson unless otherwise credited. We thank all who gave permission for their photographs to be used, and are particularly grateful to David Whiteside and Tony Smith of the World Ship Photo Library; and to Peter Newall, Ivor Rooke, William Schell, George Scott and the museums and institutions listed for help in finding photographs.

In researching captions, sources have included the *Registers* of William Schell and Tony Starke, *Lloyd's Register, Lloyd's Confidential Index, Lloyd's War Losses, Mercantile Navy Lists,* and *Marine News.* Use of the facilities of the World Ship Society's Central Record, the Guildhall Library and Lloyd's Register of Shipping are gratefully acknowledged. Particular thanks also to William Schell and John Bartlett for information, to Heather Fenton for editorial work, and to Marion Clarkson for accountancy services.

Trader Navigation
A fleet list and brief history by C.F. Godwin appeared in *Marine News* for July 1963, and further details came from a fleet list compiled by Len Grey and now in the World Ship Society's collection. Also consulted were *Shipwreck Index of the British Isles: the East Coast of England* by R. & B. Larn (Lloyd's Register, London, 1997). Background on the grain trade and Bunge came from *The World Grain Trade* by Tom Sewell (Woodhead-Faulkner, London, 1992), and the racier but more revealing *Merchants of Grain* by Dan Morgan (Weidenfeld & Nicolson, London, 1979).

IMPERIAL STAR class
Ships' careers were taken largely from *Blue Star* by Tony Atkinson and Kevin O'Donoghue (World Ship Society, Kendal, 1985).

The ups and downs of BARON VERNON
Colin Campbell searched the records of the Clyde Navigation Trust in the Mitchell Library, Glasgow. Further details of the salvage and career of the BARON VERNON are taken with the author's permission from *Head Line* by W.J. Harvey (World Ship Society, Kendal, 1990).

Pilgrim ships for Mecca
This feature was inspired by an article on pilgrim ships written by the late Colonel Robert Gabriel for *The Syren & Shipping* in July 1966. Long recognised as the expert on Eastern shipping, a number of the Colonel's excellent photos have been used, courtesy of Ambrose Greenway. Thanks also to Raisuke Numata and Peter Leggatt for their help with information.

PILGRIM SHIPS FOR MECCA
Peter Newall

The Prophet Muhammad, the founder of Islam, was born about 570 in Mecca, a town in western Saudi Arabia. This religious centre, with the cube shaped building the Ka'bah at its core, is the holiest city of Islam. To this remote part of the world, it is the duty of every adult Muslim to attempt a pilgrimage, or Hadj, at least once in his or her lifetime. The Hadj is also the fifth of the fundamental Muslim practices known as the Five Pillars of Islam. Before the Jeddah international airport was built in the 1980s, the only way to get to Mecca was by sea to the nearby port of Jeddah. For centuries, millions of pilgrims have poured into Mecca, many having suffered great hardships on the way.

Like the emigrant trade to the Americas, shipowners soon recognised the great opportunity for making a profit in the transportation of large numbers of pilgrims who require little in terms of creature comforts – these passengers also did not complain as discomfort was seen as part of the pilgrim's ordeal. One of the first steamship owners to enter this trade soon after the opening of the Suez Canal was Alfred Holt, whose cargo ships made regular calls at Jeddah on their way to China via the Malayan peninsula – including the Dutch East Indies, this was a vast Muslim region. The Ocean Steamship Company vessels were built to passenger certificate standard and could carry 1,000 pilgrims per voyage as deck passengers in 'tween deck space.

Prior to arrival at Jeddah, the 'tween decks had to be cleaned (a major problem if the cargo was coal), and a multitude of temporary fixtures put in place including portable latrines, ventilation windsails (the heat in the Red Sea is unbearable at any time of year), liferafts, and safety ropes. Water and firewood for cooking (another major hazard) was also provided. At Jeddah, pilgrims were usually ferried to the ship in dhows. Most of the time during the voyage, the pilgrims remained below deck reading the Koran or taking prayers.

Blue Funnel's connection with the Malayan Hadj trade came to an end in 1952, when the company chartered the pilgrim space on their 2,500-capacity pilgrim ship TYNDAREUS (11,347/1916) to an Indonesian Government sponsored organisation. By 1958, the Indonesians asked for a better ship, and Blue Funnel bought the troopship EMPIRE ORWELL which had been built in 1935 as the German passenger liner PRETORIA. Her conversion into the partially air-conditioned GUNUNG DJATI with accommodation for 106 first class passengers and 2,000 pilgrims in special beds and spaces, was the beginning of the modern pilgrim era (see page 1). This ship, which was bought by the Indonesian Government in 1962, lasted until 1987, albeit latterly in the Indonesian Navy.

Holt's Malayan traffic rights were transferred to the China Navigation Company in 1953, and the company placed their relatively new ANKING (seen below leaving Singapore on a Hadj voyage) and ANSHUN on the service. This 6,100gt pair had been built in 1950 and 1951 respectively for the emigrant trade between Penang, Singapore and South China which failed to materialise because of the troubles in the region. In 1960, ANKING was replaced by the KUALA LUMPUR, the former British India troopship DILWARA which was able to carry over 2,000 pilgrims. China Navigation withdrew from the Hadj business in 1970 and the ANKING was sold as KLIAS to the Straits Steamship Co. Ltd. where she stayed until her sale for scrap in 1976.

THE INDIANS AND THE MOGULS

Prior to independence, Hadj traffic in India was controlled by so called Hadj committees, and pilgrims could only travel from Karachi, Bombay or Calcutta – this provided the shipping lines with great commercial opportunities and bitter rivalry soon followed.

JALADURGA (top)
Barclay, Curle & Co. Ltd., Glasgow; 1910, 3,958 gt, 391 feet

The foundation of the Scindia Steam Navigation Company in March 1919 has been seen as the start of modern Indian shipping and a major step towards Indian independence. Flying the Scindia flag with a red swastika, an ancient Indian symbol (the Nazi symbol was an inverted version), the new company was soon a thorn in the side of the British operators in India. By 1933, with an increased fleet, they bought two former British India coastal ships COCONADA and EDAVANA, and renamed them JALADURGA and JALAGOPAL. The former was used primarily on the Rangoon-Coromandal passenger service, and both ships also carried Hadj pilgrims. JALADURGA was requisitioned as a military store ship in 1941 and after the war was handed back to her owners in Bombay, where she was scrapped in 1955. *[National Maritime Museum]*

EL HIND (middle)
Lithgows Ltd., Port Glasgow; 1938, 5,319gt, 400 feet

The success of the JALADURGA and JALAGOPAL in the pilgrim trade prompted Scindia to order two purpose-built ships for their newly-formed Hadj Line. These ships would also compete head on with their great rival, the British-owned Mogul Line. The first to arrive in 1937 was EL MADINA from Barclay, Curle – designed also for the Indian coastal run, she carried twelve first-class and 33 second-class passengers, as well as 850 unberthed pilgrims, or 2,000 deck passengers on very short journeys. EL HIND followed the next year and, during the 1938-39 pilgrim season, the company carried a fifth of the Bombay-Jeddah traffic. Scindia suspended the service the following season, however, as a protest against Mogul Line being awarded 75% of the traffic, but by now war of a different kind was in the air and the service ceased. On Friday, 14th April 1944, EL HIND was unfortunately in Bombay docks when the FORT STIKINE, loaded with 1,400 tons of explosives, caught fire and blew up, with devastating consequences. EL HIND was one of many ships destroyed that day. With the loss of EL MADINA the same year, Scindia planned two post war replacement 8,500 gt pilgrim ships with the same names as the pre-war pair but, following independence in 1947, these two ships were placed on the India-UK run as JALAZAD and JALJAWAHAR. In 1961 they became

STATE OF BOMBAY and STATE OF MADRAS. *[Peter Newall collection]*

RIZWANI (bottom)
Lithgows Ltd., Port Glasgow; 1930, 5,448gt, 410 feet

One of the oldest registered Indian shipping companies, the Bombay and Persia Steamship Company was formed in 1877 by four muslim merchants in Bombay. Initially the company operated between Bombay and the Persian Gulf only, but later became a major player in the seasonal pilgrim traffic. British controlled from 1913, in the 1920s the line ordered a number of new ships, including the Lithgow-built pair RAHMANI and RIZWANI of 1928 and 1930. These coal burners were followed in 1934 by the slightly larger ISLAMI and eventually the company, which became known as Mogul Line in 1939, had the virtual monopoly of the Bombay pilgrim trade much to the chagrin of Scindia. RIZWANI remained in the fleet until 1959 when she was scrapped in India. Her sister was sunk by a submarine in the Gulf of Aden in July 1943. [Peter Newall collection]

MOZAFFARI (top)
Lithgows Ltd., Port Glasgow; 1948, 7,024gt, 435 feet

With Scindia no longer interested in the pilgrim trade after independence, Mogul Line's two new Lithgow-built passenger ships MOHAMMEDI and MOZAFFARI had the Indian and Pakistani pilgrim trade almost to themselves when they arrived in 1947 and 1948 respectively. With a service speed of 14.5 knots, these rather ungainly ships with tiny funnels offered much improved accommodation for 62 first-class passengers and 1,390 pilgrims, all with individual berths on two 'tween decks. Off-season, they ran between India, Pakistan and Red Sea ports. In 1950 they were chartered by the International Refugee Organisation for a single voyage each with emigrants for Australia, and renamed OCEAN TRIUMPH and OCEAN VICTORY respectively. The Indian Government gained overall control of Mogul Line in 1960, with a complete take-over in 1975. Two years later MOZAFFARI was sent to Bombay breakers, followed by her sister in 1978. [Col. Robert Gabriel, Ambrose Greenway collection]

SAUDI (middle)
Lithgows Ltd., Port Glasgow; 1956, 5,973gt, 426 feet (overall)

Yet another product of Lithgows, SAUDI was a handsome ship, slightly smaller than the 1940s pair, with space for 12 first class and 900 pilgrims. The entrances for the pilgrim 'tween deck space were the masthouses on the upper deck. On 25th June 1973, on a voyage from Aqaba to Cochin with phosphate rock, her cargo shifted in heavy seas off Cape Guardafui, Somalia. She capsized and sank so quickly that there was no time to launch any lifeboats and everyone had to jump overboard. Thirty nine out of the ninety eight crew and family lost their lives in the tragedy. [Col. Robert Gabriel, Ambrose Greenway collection]

NOOR JEHAN (bottom)
Soc. Española de Construcción Naval, Bilbao, Spain; 1959, 14,569gt, 556 feet (overall)

In the mid 1950s, the famous Spanish company Ybarra y Compañía ordered two new liners for their South American service to replace their ageing pair of former American President Line vessels. These two 21 knot ships, CABO SAN VICENTE and CABO SAN ROQUE, were probably the finest Spanish liners ever built and were outstanding not only for their attractive exterior design but also for their superb facilities for 189 cabin and 652 tourist class passengers. By 1975, with rising fuel costs and a changing market, their owners were unable to make them pay, and CABO SAN

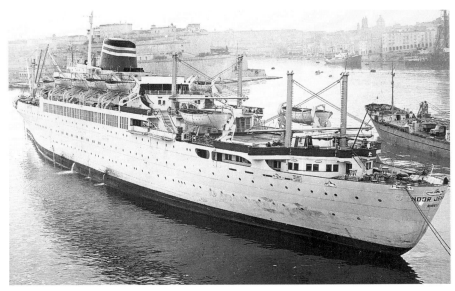

VICENTE was sold to Mogul Line for use as the pilgrim ship NOOR JEHAN – at last Mogul had a fully air-conditioned ship. Laid up at Bombay in 1984, she was scrapped the following year, the last of the Mogul Line pilgrim ships. [Peter Newall collection]

THE NEW MUSLIM STATE

The newly independent Pakistan had to wait four years after independence before they had their own Hadj company to carry the vast multitude of muslims living in West and East Pakistan. With ships bearing the distinctive funnel marking of a green band with crescent moon and stars, the Pan-Islamic Steamship Co. Ltd. of Karachi was founded in 1951. After the breakaway of East Pakistan in 1971 (forming Bangladesh), the company came under the control of the Pakistani Government in 1974, but was denationalised in 1980.

SAFINA-E-ARAB (1) (above)
Harland & Wolff Ltd., Belfast; 1912, 8,648gt, 475 feet
One of the first in the new Pan-Islamic fleet was the former OXFORDSHIRE, built for Bibby Line in 1912. Easily recognisable as a Bibby liner by the four tall masts, she had a distinguished career as a hospital ship in both world wars. The last of the 'Burma boats' with a counter stern, she was built for her owner's Birkenhead-Rangoon service, with accommodation for 295 first class passengers. During the First World War, as HM HOSPITAL SHIP No. 1, she carried over 53,000 wounded personnel, the highest of any hospital ship in the war. Converted to burn oil in 1920, she remained on the Burma route until 1939 when she again became a hospital ship. Post-war, she carried emigrants and troops until her sale to the Pakistanis in 1951 as SAFINA-E-ARAB (Ship of the Arabs). She was broken up at Karachi in 1958. *[Peter Newall collection]*

SAFINA-E-MURAD (opposite bottom)
Reiherstieg Schiffswerft, Hamburg, Germany; 1920, 7,690gt, 426 feet
In 1951, Pan-Islamic also bought a German built liner, which had had a chequered and interesting career. Renamed SAFINA-E-MURAD, she had been launched as MARIE WOERMANN in 1916 for the Woermann-Linie of Hamburg for their West African service, but war intervened and work on her ceased. In the same year, the Woermann family sold out to a consortium of HAPAG, Norddeutscher Lloyd and Hugo Stinnes and as a result the unfinished vessel was renamed WADAI. Allocated after the war initially to Britain, she was completed in 1920, and the following year was sold to Royal Rotterdam Lloyd. Renamed TJERIMAI, she remained on the Dutch East Indies service until the arrival of the new motorships DEMPO and BALOERAN in 1930. After a period of lay-up, she became the Egyptian EL NIL in 1933 and had her first taste of the pilgrim trade. In 1943, she too became a hospital ship and eventually a British transport vessel. Able to carry 1,000 deck passengers, she remained with Pan-Islamic for only three years before being broken up at Gadani Beach in 1954. *[Col. Robert Gabriel, Ambrose Greenway collection]*

SAFINA-E-NUSRAT (top)
William Denny & Bros., Dumbarton; 1914, 7,821gt, 467 feet
SAFINA-E-MURAD was replaced in 1953 by another ex 'Burma boat', SAFINA-E-NUSRAT. Completed as BURMA in 1914 for Henderson's Glasgow-Burma service, this handsome passenger-cargo liner carried just over 100 passengers and remained with Hendersons for 35 years. Sold in 1949 to a Panamanian-registered, Italian-based company, as FLORENTIA she was used as an emigrant carrier to South America and Australia. In 1957, she was scrapped at Karachi. *[Eric Johnson collection]*

SAFINA-E- HUJJAJ (below)
Blohm & Voss, Hamburg, Germany; 1935, 17,528gt, 604 feet.
By 1958, Pan-Islamic chartered EMPIRE ORWELL for six months to carry pilgrims between Karachi and Jeddah. For some reason, they never bought the ship but not long after Blue Funnel converted her into GUNUNG DJATI, the Pakistanis bought the even larger troopship EMPIRE FOWEY in 1960 and renamed her SAFINA-E- HUJJAJ. Ordered for HAPAG as POTSDAM, in the 1934 reorganisation of German shipping she was sold to Norddeutscher Lloyd for their express Bremerhaven-Far East service. Like her running mate SCHARNHORST, she was turbo-electric, with a maximum speed of 23 knots – joining the ship in Genoa, it was possible to reach Shanghai in 21 days. During the war, she initially served as a naval accommodation ship at Hamburg. In 1942, work was planned for her conversion into an aircraft carrier but this did not happen and she became an accommodation ship at Gotenhafen (Gydnia). At the end of the war, she was awarded to Britain as a prize and carried troops as EMPIRE JEWEL. Renamed EMPIRE FOWEY in 1946, her conversion into a permanent trooper took three years from 1947 to 1950, when she emerged with accommodation for over 1,600 officers and men. As a pilgrim ship, she carried 166 first-class, 295 second-class, and 2,141 pilgrims, some in dormitories and others on deck. With her speed, she was also able to transport five full loads of pilgrims in the 66 days available. Although primarily a pilgrim ship, she was also used on routes from Pakistan to Hong Kong and East Africa, and was eventually sent to the breakers in 1976. *[Col. Robert Gabriel, Ambrose Greenway collection]*

SAFINA-E-ARAFAT (top)
Chantiers et Ateliers de Saint Nazaire (Penhoët), France; 1952, 9,499gt, 479 feet (overall)
This pilgrim carrier had only a brief stay with Pan-Islamic. The last in a series of three similar-sized passenger-cargo ships built for Chargeur Reunis' West African service (the first two came from Swan Hunter), she started life as GENERAL LECLERC. Partially air-conditioned, she carried 561 passengers. In 1965, she was transferred to a new subsidiary, Nouvelle Compagnie de Paquebots (CNP), which was jointly owned by Chargeur Reunis and Paquet. In 1970, she was bought by Pan-Islamic and named SAFINA-E-ARAFAT, but later that year, this was changed to SAFINA-E-SIAHAT. Laid up in January 1971, apparently after a fire, she was sold for scrap in September. *[Peter Newall collection]*

SAFINA-E-ARAB (2) (middle)
Soc.Española de Const. Naval, Cadiz, Spain; 1961, 8,477gt, 461 feet (overall)
This motorship, the last of the Pan-Islamic pilgrim ships, was purpose built at Cadiz to serve the East Pakistan market and was based at Chittagong. With a service speed of 15 knots, she could carry three full loads to Jeddah during the pilgrim season. As usual, over 1,000 pilgrims were provided with space in the 'tween decks, and facilities on board included two hospitals, one for each sex. During the war of independence in 1971, she carried evacuees from Chittagong to West Pakistan and, after the cessation of Bangladesh, she

was based in Karachi. In 1996 she was demolished at Gadani Beach. *[Col. Robert Gabriel, Ambrose Greenway collection]*

THE BANGLADESHIS, INDONESIANS AND EGYPTIANS

HIZBUL BAHR (bottom)
Chantiers et Ateliers de Saint Nazaire (Penhoët), Saint Nazaire, France; 1953, 12,457gt, 532 feet (overall)
In 1977 the Bangladesh Shipping Corporation bought a former fully air-conditioned French liner for a passenger service between Chittagong and Dubai. Renamed HIZBUL BAHR (Sentinel of the Sea), she also carried Hadj passengers during the pilgrim season. Originally

GENERAL MANGIN, she and her near sister JEAN MERMOZ operated a passenger-cargo service to West Africa and the Congo for her Marseilles owners, Compagnie Fraissinet et Cyprien Fabre. In 1965 she was transferred to Nouvelle Compagnie de Paquebots (CNP). Sold to the Philippine President Lines in 1969 as PRESIDENT for a Philippines-Japan service, three years later she was bought by Cia. De Nav. Abeto S.A., a Panamanian registered, Hong Kong-

owned company, which included in its fleet a number of former French liners. Placed on the Singapore-Fremantle run as EASTERN QUEEN, she remained for five years until she was sold to Bangladesh. In 1981 she was taken over by the Bangladesh Navy as an oceanographic ship SHAHEED SALASMUDDIN, but used as a pilgrim carrier until scrapped in 1985. *[Ambrose Greenway collection]*

KOAN MARU

Mitsubishi Jukogyo K.K., Nagasaki, Japan;1936, 7,079gt, 418 feet

Until the purchase of GUNUNG DJATI in 1962, Indonesian pilgrims had to travel in 'tween deck space on Dutch ships operating to Indonesia, or in chartered vessels, one of which was the Japanese ferry KOAN MARU. This attractive ship had such an eventful career that a whole book could be written on her history. Built for the Ministry of Railway Transport, she and her sister operated the overnight service between Shimonoseki and Pusan. Carrying 350 passengers, they were not only fast (23 knots), but also had air-conditioning in all cabins – a unique feature in the 1930s. Despite mine damage, she was one of the few Japanese passenger vessels to survive the war. In the late 1940s and 1950s, she was used on numerous trooping and repatriation voyages and, between 1959 and 1967, was chartered by the Indonesians as a pilgrim ship. After a fire in Brawan Bay in 1967, she returned to Yokohama and was scrapped three years later at Mihara. *[Col. Robert Gabriel, Ambrose Greenway collection]*

BELLE ABETO

Ateliers et Chantiers de la Loire, Saint-Nazaire, France; 1951, 12,177gt, 537 feet (overall)

Between 1950 and 1954, a series of eight similar-sized passenger-cargo motorships were built for Chargeur Reunis. Three of these vessels ended up in the hands of the Abeto company and became Indonesian pilgrim ships. Two were originally LAËNNEC and CHARLES TELLIER and were completed for Compagnie Sudatlantique, a subsidiary of Chargeur Reunis, in 1952. Both ships operated on the Hamburg-River Plate service and in 1962 were transferred to Messageries Maritimes ownership and remained on the same route until their sale to Abeto in 1966 and 1967 respectively. Converted into pilgrim ships, they were renamed BELLE ABETO and LE HAVRE ABETO, and chartered to the official Indonesian pilgrim operator P.T.Perusahaan Pelajaran 'Arafat'. In 1971, BELLE ABETO, although still under the Panamanian flag, became part of the 'Arafat' fleet. On 29th July 1976, prior to a voyage to Jakarta, and whilst awaiting bunkers at the quarantine anchorage, Sasebo, Japan, she caught fire in her engine room. Two days later, she sank. Following the collapse of the 'Arafat' company in the late 1970s, her sister and MEI ABETO (ex LOUIS LUMIÈRE) were laid up at Jakarta until they were sold for scrap in 1984.

AMBULOMBO (top)
Alexander Stephen & Sons, Glasgow; 1935, 10,856gt, 464 feet

When the motorship MANOORA was delivered to the Adelaide Steamship Company in 1935, she was the first Australian coastal liner over 10,000gt. With accommodation for 250 first class and 130 second class passengers, she ran on the Sydney-Fremantle via Melbourne and Adelaide service. In 1939 she was converted into an armed merchant cruiser for the Australian Navy and operated mainly on Pacific patrols. Three years later she became a landing ship and was used to land troops on Japanese-held islands in the East Indies and Philippines. After a lengthy refit, she returned to her owners in 1949 and continued on her original run until 1961 when, as the last large coastal liner, she was bought by the Indonesian Government. Renamed AMBULOMBO, she was managed by the state run pilgrim organisation P.T. Pelayaran Nasional Indonesia. Following a brief ownership by P.T. Affan Raya as AFFAN OCEANA, in 1966 she was sold to P.T. Perusahaan Pelajaran "Arafat" and reverted back to AMBULOMBO. In 1972, she was sold to Taiwanese breakers but sank off Luzon whilst in tow by a Japanese tug. *[Peter Newall collection]*

MISR (middle)
Consolidated Steel Corporation, Wilmington, California, USA; 1943, 7,367gt, 395 feet

In the pre-Boeing 747 days, ships used to run regularly between Port Tewfik at Suez and Jeddah during the pilgrim season. Originally, the main operator was the Khedivial Mail Line, which along with other Egyptian companies was nationalised to form the United Arab Maritime Company in 1960. Two of the Egyptian pilgrim ships were originally laid down as US C1-type cargo ships, but completed as military landing vessels able to carry large numbers of troops. Thirteen of these were built, and chartered by the British Government. Laid down with CAPE names, they were given EMPIRE nomenclatures on completion. MISR was first CAPE ST. ROQUE and then EMPIRE MACE. In 1944, she was transferred with eight of this type to the Royal Navy, and renamed HMS GALTEE MORE which, like the names given to the others, was a Derby winner. Shortly after the end of the war, she and a sister (completed as EMPIRE ARQUEBUS) were sold to the Egyptian company Société Misr de Navigation Maritime as MISR and AL SUDAN (ie. Egypt and Sudan). They were ideal for the transportation of large numbers of workers and, of course, pilgrims. Both were sold for demolition in the early 1980s. *[Alex Duncan collection]*

GUMHURYAT MISR (bottom)
Cammell Laird & Co. Ltd. Birkenhead; 1928, 7,831gt, 420 feet

LADY NELSON and LADY RODNEY were the only survivors at the end of the Second World War of the five LADY ships built for

Canadian National (West Indies) Steamships in 1928 and 1929. Designed to carry passengers and cargo between Canada and the West Indies, these handsome white ships were immensely popular in their day and played a major role in the development of cruising in the Caribbean. During the war LADY NELSON became Canada's first hospital ship. After her return to the West Indies run, the service incurred large losses, and both vessels were sold to the Khedivial Mail Line in 1953. LADY RODNEY was fitted to carry 1,300 pilgrims as the MECCA and was used primarily as a pilgrim ship on the North Africa-Jeddah route. LADY NELSON was renamed GUMHURYAT MISR (Republic of Egypt) and refitted to carry 120 first class and 130 tourist class for an unsuccessful New York service. After use as an emigrant ship, her passenger capacity was increased to almost 1,500, and she spent most of her remaining years plying the pilgrim trades between Syria, Egypt and Jeddah, with her name changed to ALWADI (Nile Valley) in 1960. In December 1965 she struck a submerged object in Alexandria and was subsequently laid up. She was reportedly sold for scrap in 1976, but remained in *Lloyd's Register* until 1980. *[Peter Newall collection]*